Speaking of Art

Speaking of Art 1958–2008

Selections from the Archives of American Art Oral History Collection

Archives of American Art, Smithsonian Institution | Winterhouse Editions, 2008
Published with the support of the Dedalus Foundation, Inc.

6   *Introduction*

Inter-views

8   *Abraham Walkowitz*
14   *Charles Burchfield*
20   *Isamu Noguchi*
24   *Stuart Davis*
32   *Burgoyne Diller*
38   *Dorothea Lange*
44   *A. Hyatt Mayor*
50   *Edith Gregor Halpert*
56   *Jacob Lawrence*
62   *Emmy Lou Packard*
70   *Lee Krasner*
76   *Robert Motherwell*
82   *Leo Castelli*
88   *Robert Rauschenberg*
92   *Al Held*
96   *Katharine Kuh*
102 *Tom Wesselmann*
106 *Agnes Martin*
112 *Sheila Hicks*
120 *Jay DeFeo*
126 *Robert C. Scull*
134 *Chuck Close*
142 *Ken Shores*
146 *Maya Lin*
152 *Guerrilla Girls*

Perhaps no experience is as profoundly visceral for the historian than to read and listen to individuals recount the stories of their lives and careers in an interview. Although the written document can provide extraordinary insight, the intimacy of the one-on-one interview offers a candor and immediacy rarely encountered on the page.

Introduction

In 1958, with great prescience, the Archives of American Art initiated an oral history program that quickly became a cornerstone of our mission. With seed money from the Ford Foundation, the Archives set out to record the life stories of the artists, collectors, dealers, and others who have shaped the visual arts in the United States. Today, fifty years and three thousand interviews later, the Archives' oral history program continues to build upon that visionary goal and has become a vital resource for the study of art, cultural, and social history.

A quick glance at this book's contents provides a snapshot of the catholic nature of the oral history program. From Abraham Walkowitz to Robert Rauschenberg, Lee Krasner to Maya Lin, inclusiveness and diversity have been the defining standards that have guided the program. That the program remains vigorous is demonstrated by the inclusion of an interview completed just this year with the activist artists' collective, the Guerrilla Girls.

While this publication celebrates the golden anniversary of the Archives' oral history program, it is not intended as an exercise in nostalgia. In reading these interviews, one realizes that the challenges and struggles that artists faced in the past are not that dissimilar to those confronting artists today. And if history is there to teach us, what better way to learn about the art world than directly through the words of some of our nation's most distinguished artists, curators, patrons, and dealers.

The oral history program has been made possible by the generosity of many funders. In addition to the Ford Foundation, major benefactors include the New York State Council on the Arts, the Pew Charitable Trust, the Mark Rothko Foundation, and the Pasadena Art Alliance. Today this project remains remarkably vigorous, thanks to support from the Terra Foundation for American Art, the Brown Foundation of Houston, the Widgeon Point Charitable Foundation, the Art Dealers Association of America, and in particular Nanette L. Laitman, who has recently funded nearly 150 interviews with American craft artists.

I am deeply grateful to the many people who have worked so hard to make this publication a success. At the Archives, I wish to thank our oral history program assistant Emily Hauck, interns Jessica Davis and Lindsey Kempton, and in particular our Curator of Manuscripts, Liza Kirwin. Liza not only undertook the daunting task of selecting and excerpting interviews for the book from among a field of three thousand, but she also wrote the introductions to each entry and selected the accompanying photographs. Her comprehensive knowledge of the oral history collection and current stewardship of the program have ensured that a thoughtfully diverse range of interviews is included here.

I would also like to thank our guest editor Susan F. Rossen for the consummate skill and sensitivity she has brought to bear in shaping the texts that appear here. Her deft touch allows the individual voice and cadence of these interviews to spring to life on the page. Winterhouse Editions is responsible for the book's elegant and lively design.

Crucial funding for this publication was received from the Dedalus Foundation. I am most grateful to the Board of Directors of the Foundation, in particular members Jack Flam and Morgan Spangle, for their support and advocacy of this project. Additional backing came through the Edgar P. Richardson Publications Fund of the Archives of American Art, a recently established fund named in honor of one of our founders.

But the real heroes of this book are the thousands of individuals who have participated in our oral history program over the past fifty years. Their willingness to give freely of their time and their memories has not only added depth to the collections of the Archives of American Art but will continue to enrich the documentary record of the visual arts in the United States for generations to come.

John W. Smith has been the director of the Archives of American Art since 2006.

Abraham Walkowitz

1878 – 1965

The Archives of American Art began its oral history program
in late 1958 with an interview of the painter Abraham
Walkowitz conducted by Abram Lerner and Bartlett Cowdrey.
Unfortunately, the audio recording no longer exists. While we
have lost this rare example of Walkowitz's voice—the rich flavor
of his Russian Jewish accent and his humorous modulations
of tone—its echo comes through in print.

In this excerpt, Walkowitz talks about his embrace of
modern art, his friendship with the artist Max Weber, and the
exhibition he organized of his art at the Julius Haas Gallery,
New York, in 1908.

Abraham Walkowitz in his studio with paintings, 1908.
Photograph by Carl Shulman. Abraham Walkowitz papers, 1904–1966.

Abram Lerner: Well, Walky, your background had included studying at the National Academy and Art Students League. So what attracted you to this new way of looking and seeing?

Abraham Walkowitz: Because I felt the reality of it. I prepared myself in a way to see it. I had seen the Monet exhibition ... in the old Parke-Bernet Gallery on 23rd Street.... It included views of a church [Rheims Cathedral] painted at different hours.... I had seen exhibitions at the Durand-Ruel Gallery; they had modern art. I was scared, but it all impressed me as being very, very logical.... It stimulated me. It made me see. In fact, the trip to Italy [in 1907], looking at Giotto, Cimabue, the primitives: we couldn't see them here. Now we have primitives, but not at that time. It certainly opened my eyes, but I was ready to see.

... I went to exhibitions at the Louvre, and I attended concerts. I was in the spirit. Paris was really Paris at that time. There were not many Americans. I lived, of course, in the American quarter, and I didn't learn French. I had to speak to the French in English. They wanted to learn English from me, and I had forgotten it. When I came back to New York, I found I had improved my English in Paris. I studied, of course, at the Académie Julian. For a short time I went to the Académie des Beaux-Arts, but I didn't like it. That's where I met [Max] Weber, in the classes there, and we became very good friends. Then I decided to go to Italy, it was just at Easter. And Weber followed me a couple of days later. He just happened to find one of those excursions, you know, one of those cheap excursions. Weber and I went to Florence and Venice together and then to a little country place in Anticoli Corrado, it's near Rome, about an hour and a half away. I remained in Italy, and Weber went back to Paris. I was to go back too, but I received a letter from my sister that my mother took sick, so I had to come back...earlier than I expected.

What happened after you came back to the United States in 1908, after the first trip?

I found it very, very hard to get an exhibition.

I went from one gallery to another to see if I could arrange an exhibition.

They looked at the drawings and said, "My dear Mr. Walkowitz, you don't expect us to show these works of art. We'll lose our clients." Of course at that time, in 1908, there were only about eight galleries, not like the 220 now. I was discouraged. I walked up and down Madison Avenue, and decided I would play the violin. I was not a master player, but I had played for some years. But I didn't like…the sound of the violin, it hurt my ears.… I used to play duets with this man, Julius Haas. I lost track of him. But I walked down Madison Avenue, between 59th and 60th Streets, and I saw a man standing in his store; a little gallery. He had no pictures, except in back, but he used to frame photographs and Gainsborough prints. He had fairly nice clients. And he stopped me, "Hello, Walky." "Hello, Julius. Listen, Julius, say yes," when he showed me the back gallery.… "You have a nice little place here. You say yes to me, and I'll tell you what it is." He says, "Yes." "Do you own this?" He says, "Yes." So I said, "Listen. I'd like to have this gallery for about a month or six weeks." He says, "You can have it. I'll take all the things out; you can have it tomorrow." I said, "I can't have it by tomorrow, but in about a week. I have to frame those things, mount them, mat them and so on." So about a week after that I arranged an exhibition of drawings and paintings, and that was the first exhibition held here of modern art. In 1908, the end of January.… And the newspapers just roasted me.… Rehn's father was a critic on the *Herald Tribune*. He was a marine painter, but he was also a critic. And he just slapped me silly: "Of no importance." But one person, who had just started to write about art a few months before, it was a woman critic, I've forgotten her name. About that time, she had written a book, I believe, on William Blake, and you have to know something to do this, so she was very good.

Bartlett Cowdrey: Elisabeth Luther Carey.

Yes. She gave me a very nice criticism. But the others just roasted me. But one, DuBois, who was a critic on the *Journal*, he commented that the "first Fauve madman like Matisse, is Walkowitz with his monstrosities on the walls of Julius Haas [Gallery]." This brought a lot of people to the show. You know, like they went to see the gorillas and monkeys in the zoo. They came. Crowds. Crowds after crowds. I had to extend the exhibition for another three weeks. It attracted great attention, no sales, except good roastings. Of course I was discouraged, I knew my subject well, I was a good fighter. I knew at that time Emma Goldman. You know, I was a radical. I was fearless. There were no "ifs" with me. I knew I was right. In order to be right, you must first always be wrong, and then you are right. I always say there are three things we have to go through in life: first state is fear; second state is sneer; third state is cheer. First they fear an idea, it disturbs their equilibrium, so they fear it. Second state is, they say, "Only a few cranks like it, so it's not popular." Then when everybody begins to like the thing, they all cheer.... In politics and in all progress we have to go through those three states.

I was a good fighter, and I was fighting day and night at the gallery. Weekends, I was invited into society, to all the rich millionaires, at tables, to talk. And they invited professors from Columbia — history of art — and so on. So I made nothing out of them at the table. Because I knew they were laughing at it [Walkowitz's art]. So when they were laughing at it, I said, "The joke is on you."

The following year, Weber came to New York. I met him on his first day.... I went to Brooklyn to see him at his father's place. I had known already where his father lived, because we [Weber and himself] used to correspond, and I told him, when I came from Italy, "I'll see your father, and I'll give regards from Max." His father and mother were very religious. He couldn't even show a drawing at home. So I said, "Max, you come to my studio." I had a studio on 23rd Street, right near the Parke-Bernet at that time. So he came the following day, and I had a cot, and by pulling out the cot this way, we slept in one cot. Almost three months he was with me. I had to do something else in order to earn a little money, and he was there in my studio, and he had to go out and find out for himself what I told him, "You go into the galleries." I wanted him to get the same experience that I got. He became discouraged, and said, "Oh, I'd like to go back to Europe. I can't take this. There's nothing, nothing. I can't arrange an exhibition. They don't even want to look at photographs." So I went to Julius Haas, with whom I had had that exhibition. I said, "Julius, you must do me a favor." He says, "You know, I lost many customers on account of you. There was a lot of noise, and the people and I lost a lot of trade." I said, "Julius, you're a sport. Do me a favor. He's a very good artist. I believe in him. Give him an exhibition." I pleaded with him until he decided. And I took Weber over to the gallery, and [Haas] gave him an exhibition. Otherwise he wouldn't have had an exhibition. And through me he met a collector [Mrs. Nathan Miller] who became his lifelong friend, who helped him, gave him money, and bought from him.... That's the way it happened. Then, later on, 1911, I was picked up by [the dealer Alfred] Stieglitz.

13

Abraham Walkowitz

Charles Burchfield

1893 – 1967

In 1959 John D. Morse interviewed painter Charles Burchfield
at his studio in Gardenville, New York. Burchfield, who is
best known for his lyrical evocations of nature in watercolor,
often wrote his poetic observations in free verse on the back
of his works. In this excerpt, Burchfield reads his own written
descriptions of his watercolors and comments on the future
of art in America. He also talks about his aversion to teaching.
The interview was funded by the Ford Foundation.

John D. Morse: Incidentally, Mr. Burchfield, while I have this Whitney [Museum of American Art] catalogue in my hand here [for a 1956 retrospective exhibition], as a writer I want to tell you how much I enjoyed and how much I congratulate you on these comments. Did you have much difficulty writing them? Did you write each one of these for each picture, or did your journal sometimes supply you with this information?

Charles Burchfield: Well, some of it, of course. But I used to do that more than I do now.... I would write out what I felt about the subject and then write it on the back of the watercolor.... Like the one now— is *Crabbed Old Age* reproduced in there?

Let's see, that would be about when?

1917. Here it is.

Yes...

[Reading] "Crabbed old age sits in front of her black doorway without hope for the future, brooding. Spiders lurk in dark corners. The dying plants reflect her mood. The romantic outer moon rises just the same."

Well, then, that you had written on the back of that watercolor itself?

Yes.

Well, then, many of the pictures of yours that are in museums and in private collections have these phrases, these descriptive phrases, on the back?

Yes, unfortunately...

But they're concealed, of course?

... I mounted them, but I would generally write on the back of the mount.

Oh, I see.

Now this I had a description for.

The Song of the Katydids [1917]?

[Reading] "A stagnant August morning during the drought season, as the pitiless sun mounts into the mid-morning sky, and the insect chorus commences, the katydids and locusts predominating. Their monotonous, mechanical, brassy rhythms soon pervade the whole air, combining with heat waves of the sun, and saturating trees and houses and sky."

Well, that's wonderful! Why haven't you written more?

Well, at one time I did think I was going to be a writer, when I was in high school, and even the early years in art school I thought I was going to be a nature writer in somewhat the sense, you know, that [Edwin Way] Teale writes, and Harold Borland, and so forth. And if I did anything with art work, I would make my own illustrations. But I soon realized that my outlook was visual rather than otherwise. . . .

Well, what do you think might be the future of art in America, or the western world? We seem to agree that abstraction has more or less won its battle.

It's won its battle, and now it is repeating itself over and over and over again. I haven't seen anything new—and I do look at the magazines and so forth—and I haven't seen anything new in the last fifteen or twenty years. They'll have an article and they'll say, "Here's a brand new talent," maybe from England or France, or so on. It's the same old formula repeated over and over again. It isn't new. And I just wouldn't—all you can hope is that the artists will sometime again turn their attention back to humanity and the world of nature. How it's going to be done I wouldn't have any idea.

Those, incidentally, are almost the identical words of your good friend Mr. Edward Hopper; he said to me the other day that he's convinced that [art] has to turn back to nature.

Yes. There's no place else to go. And they don't seem to know it. They don't seem to know that they've said it, that it's been said. But the world of nature—now one of the arguments is that the camera has replaced the artist in reproducing people, portraits, and pictures, and so forth, and that it is no longer necessary to go to nature or to people for subject matter. Well, I think that if this world lasts for a million years or two million years, or more, that never can you exhaust the subject matter of humanity or nature. It's simply inexhaustible. I feel about my own work, for example, my interest is more in nature now than in man-made things; I don't know how much time I've got left, but I'd like to have

Charles Burchfield

at least another lifetime like I've had, to say what I want to say about nature. I just don't think I can ever get it said. There just isn't time…

What about teaching, Mr. Burchfield? I notice that you've done considerable, if not sustained, teaching, lecturing, and so on in recent years. Do you enjoy that?

No.

You don't?

No. I hope I never will do it again.

You're through with it?

Yes.… I did it reluctantly, and I don't feel that I was a good teacher. For example, you asked me…why did I like watercolor over any other medium, and I told you I didn't know, which is true, because I've used it ever since I was a child—it never presented any problems. It's as easy for me to work in watercolors as for the ordinary person who isn't an artist to use pencil or pen. There's no thought required. The only thought that is required is what I'm going to do, what I'm going to put down. But the putting of it down is just as simple as breathing. And that being the case, I couldn't possibly tell anybody how to paint in watercolor. And that's what they wanted to know. And lots of times…students entered my class hoping they would find out something about how to handle watercolor, and I told them: "Don't think about the medium. What you're trying to say is much more important than what you're saying it with. And if you're thinking about what you are trying to express, you may use watercolor like nobody else ever used it. And that's all right as long as you say what you want to say." But I'm sure that they just thought I was being cagey, I mean that I knew these tricks and I wouldn't give them to them. And, well, I wasn't. Another thing that made me a bad teacher, I think, was I just hated to say anything nasty about anybody's work.… Some of the students would say to me, "Well, Mr. Burchfield, will you tell me what you like about my paintings and what you don't like. Why don't you take it apart and tell me what's completely wrong with it?" Well, a lot of the time, you know, I would be saying to myself, "This person has no business trying to be an artist." You know, you can't say that; I couldn't anyway. Maybe it would have been the nicest thing to do, but I just couldn't do it.... If a student has talent, many teachers pay attention to that student, and the other ones they pass by in silence. Well, I just couldn't do that, so I was quite miserable...

Yes.

I conducted a seminar for the Albright School out here and, as far as I could see, it was a complete failure. I didn't get the students' sympathy or interest. They were all interested almost entirely in abstract art and there wasn't anything I could tell them about it, really.

So you feel that you are through with teaching?

Yes, I hope I—I don't think I will ever do it again.

Charles Burchfield

Isamu Noguchi

1904–1988

In 1927, at the age of twenty-three, the Japanese-American sculptor Isamu Noguchi won a prestigious Guggenheim Fellowship to study in Paris. In this excerpt from an interview conducted by Paul Cummings in 1973, Noguchi recalls his time in Paris and his work as an apprentice in the studio of the pioneering Romanian sculptor Constantin Brancusi.

Isamu Noguchi, 1968. Photograph by Russell Lynes.
Russell Lynes papers, 1935–1986

Paul Cummings: You got the Guggenheim and went to Paris in 1927.

Isamu Noguchi: Yes. But I did not go there with the intention of meeting Brancusi. It just happened as a kind of fluke. The second day I was in Paris, I met a man—Goldman—who knew Brancusi. So when I mentioned that I had seen this exhibition ["Brancusi," Brummer Gallery, New York, November 17–December 15, 1926] and that I admired it, he asked, "Would you like to meet him?" I said, "Sure." So we walked over there, you see. That's how I met Brancusi. And that's how I asked him if I could come and hang around and help him a bit. He said, "Yes." So I'd spend half a day with him and the rest of the time I'd spend drawing at the Académie Colarossi and the Grande Chaumière. I don't know how long I was with Brancusi, maybe six months, I don't really recollect exactly how long; but it was for quite a while....

… What was the activity in Brancusi's studio? Did you cut things for him?

Yes. He showed me how to help him cut bases, for instance, out of limestone; you know, how to do this and that. I was his helper, his sort of right hand. He would give me things to do that he thought I could do. He was very kind to me. After all, I didn't ask him for anything. He didn't have to pay me. I had the Guggenheim Fellowship. I was useful. You know, he wasn't a man who was given to helping people. I mean he was rather dour, you might say. I don't think he ever had many assistants, so that it was exceptional that he even allowed me to come there…

It's curious. You were twenty years old and had studied with an academic sculptor [in 1924 Noguchi took his first sculpture class at the Leonardo da Vinci Art School on Manhattan's Lower East Side with the school's founder, Onorio Ruotolo], and all of a sudden here you were in Paris going to Collarosi and Chaumière and working with Brancusi and, I suppose, moving around and meeting other people. What was Paris like for you? I mean, this was a new country and a new language and a new atmosphere.

It was a fantastic experience for a young man like me. Of course, I wasn't the only one. I mean there were other Americans in Paris: Sandy

[Alexander] Calder, for instance, whom I soon met up with and made friends with. He went there under somewhat different circumstances. But his father was a strictly academic sculptor who [had a studio] downstairs from Ruotolo's. Sandy was a freewheeling sort of cartoonist in wire, you might say. He was making those charming circus figures floating in the air. [Calder's *Circus* is now at the Whitney Museum of American Art, New York.] I would say that Sandy was one of my early influences, in that his things were anti-gravity, you know, they were very light. I made a lot of friends there, surprisingly. Whereas previously I had very few friends, in France I suddenly came upon, you might say, people who either were like me, or whom I could accept, or who would accept me. After all, this business of any kind of separation [deriving from] discrimination didn't exist there. I don't mean to say that it existed in New York either, for that matter; I did not recognize anything like that. Although, as I say, when you enter the art world you are not in a world that is discriminatory, that's the last thing artists think about. Therefore, I say it's only in the art world that you can be free.

23

Stuart Davis

1894 – 1964

When historian Harlan B. Phillips interviewed Stuart Davis in
1962, the American modernist was a living link between his
teacher Robert Henri and the Abstract Expressionists, who then
dominated the current scene. In these excerpts, he recalls his
participation in two landmark events—the 1910 "Exhibition
of Independent Artists" (which Henri had organized) and the
1913 Armory Show—and marching with the Artists' Committee
for Action in the depths of the Depression.

Stuart Davis: Robert Henri's approach laid the foundation for being an artist. You say you want to become an artist—well, art comes from life, not from codifications of art theory. That was the basic thing, a very important thing, and a true thing besides.

◄ ◄ ◄

I was in the first Independent Show ["Exhibition of Independent Artists," Galleries at 29-31 West 35th Street, New York, April 1910] and that was another thing that was going on. This idea—it's so hard to say anything about these things today because they don't mean anything to people who didn't experience the fact that they live in a world now where there are four hundred art galleries in New York City. Anybody who has painted for two weeks can have a show, if he's got enough to pay for it. The newspaper has to print art ads on Saturday, because there isn't enough room on Sunday to do it. There was nothing like that then. There were three, or four, five, six art galleries in New York, and what an art gallery meant was Knoedler or Kraushaar, a place where certain works of European old and newer masters were shown. The people on the street never thought of going into a gallery, or anything like that, and the only Americans who showed were the academicians, who had complete control of art sales and opinion, so the idea of an Independent Show was the product of that absolute dearth. Like somebody going to art school now—I was teaching at the New School [in New York City] when the soldiers came back from Korea and had the G.I. Bill. A soldier would come in and say, "How long will it take me to get a show on 52nd Street?"

I said, "Did you draw anything yet?"
He said, "No, but how long would it take?"
I said, "I don't know, but I would think a general estimate would be about thirty years."
"Aw, are you kiddin'?"

Harlan B. Phillips: That must have gone over great!

The ordinary art student in the days of the Henri School [1909–12] wouldn't think of having a show in a gallery, because there weren't any galleries that would admit his type of stuff. He wouldn't have been around long enough. That was bad. The communication of art was a very limited, formalized and restricted monopoly—you know. So the Independent Show idea developed, and this was also Henri's idea, that everybody who had done something could [exhibit]—a show with no jury and no prizes. You say, "All these things mean nothing now." Well, then it was an amazing thing. The first Independent Show was held in 1910 down on West 35th Street. They just rented an office building of three or four stories in the middle of the block between Fifth and Sixth Avenues, hung up all those paintings, and charged admission. They got out a catalogue. That was 1910. That was Henri's response to the general atmosphere of the time, [along with] John Sloan, [William] Glackens, [Edward] Shinn, [James M.] Preston, George Luks, and Rockwell Kent, too. Kent and [George] Bellows were pupils of Henri before I got onto the scene. They'd gone to the Chase School—something like that. This very contemporary kind of response was going on—the opening of the Henri School [in 1909] and [Henri] sponsoring and getting enthusiasts for this exhibition. Sloan was always an active supporter of Henri and these ideas. Sloan used to walk in Socialist parades at one time, and both were very active in organizing the 1913 Armory Show, which was a tremendous thing. They were the active thinkers, as well as men who regarded themselves as artists, as people who were interested in whatever art is. That was it, and they were doing it in this original and creative way in terms of their own facilities and their own environment, instead of some tradition that, however it may have existed in Europe, didn't really exist here except by imitation.

[At the 1913 Armory Show], you saw any number of things that were wholly new in the way of methods and techniques of conveying ideas.

Stuart Davis

I responded immediately, and the most, to [Vincent] van Gogh and [Paul] Gauguin. I didn't have any trouble wondering, "What the hell is this?" I thought, "That's it! I have to do something like that." That poster over there—the women of whatever—that was painted in 1907 [Davis was referring to a reproduction of Pablo Picasso's *Demoiselles d'Avignon*, Museum of Modern Art, New York], and that was picked out as an example of the heralding of the Cubism idea.... There were a lot of Picasso drawings in the Armory Show that didn't mean much to me—his early Cubistic work. Of course, [Marcel Duchamp's painting] *Nude Descending a Staircase* [1912; Philadelphia Museum of Art] had a very personal aspect.... I don't think the painting specifically inspired me. It's amazing how it attracted attention here. It isn't an electric sign, or anything—but, for some reason, there was something about it. In any event, it became the star of the show in public's mind....

There were ends—call them stages, and the fact that they were contradictory developments—like Surrealism, Dadaism, Cubism, Fauvism before; and later on, German Expressionism (which actually has had a revival in the last ten years in terms of American Abstract Expressionism)—that didn't bother me. I just preferred the Cubists' structural approach to things and their more familiar daily references to known objects. The German angle never appealed to me. Postwar German Expressionism was a very hysterical business, and I never wanted to do that, never was attracted. Dadaism didn't appeal to me.... These kinds of jokes are all right. I have nothing against them. Duchamp did that type of thing, and still does: sophisticated intellectualism where making a joke takes the place of doing something. I don't want to give you the impression that I'm putting Duchamp down, because anybody who can stay around so long and do actually so few physical acts—you know, he must have something. He must have something that sticks.

But these contradictory directions didn't bother me. I just stuck to the structural principles. I thought that if you have feelings and an idea that you want to express, you have to have a regard for the terms in which it is expressed. The expression becomes a public object, a thing in itself, and it has to have its own logic and its own integrity in a completely common-sense manner, otherwise it isn't expressed. It's only a sign that somebody wanted to express something. So with the Cubist angle, the Cubist approach—just as [the subject matter of] Picasso himself, no matter what kind of work he did, always refers to something that you know about. There's always something in his pictures that indicates this world and not some other, not the insane asylum, or Sigmund Freud in Vienna, or something like that. It's always a world we know about. My nature leads me to adhere to that kind of an attitude. The current wave of Abstract Expressionism never bothered me. I know the people who do it. Some of them are good, and some of them are not. If they want to do that, fine. I don't have any talent for that kind of thing, nor do I regard it as a further development in some fruitful direction. I just don't think of it at all.

During the Depression, the New York picture was complicated by the Artists' Coordinating Committee, which had been certainly one of the first public voices to call for a municipal art center managed by artists. Did you run across the name the Artists' Committee for Action?

Yes, this committee was in the municipal art-center drive also.

In [1934] the Artists' Committee for Action… had something to do with a municipal art gallery. We had headquarters—like a loft, really— on West 15th or 16th Street, and we had meetings there. We had meetings with the mayor [Fiorello LaGuardia]. I don't recall any one meeting where we met him, but we met with somebody.… I remember one time when I was sitting down in the City Hall. I guess this was after the [Committee for Action's] parade. I was sitting right next to [the philosopher and educational theorist] John Dewey. He went along. We paraded from this place on West 15th Street all the way down to the City Hall. We had banners, pictures, slogans, etc., calling for

Stuart Davis

this municipal art gallery.... I think we were between Fifth and Sixth Avenues on 15th or 16th Street,...probably 16th Street, and there were cops all the way from Sixth Avenue to Fifth Avenue, all over the place, and fire engines out with hoses. There had been an order given that we couldn't march. There was a lot of telephoning — we already had the permit, but it had been rejected, or cancelled. Anyhow, we finally got it. In the meantime, many...who were ready to march had come to this rendezvous at some ungodly hour—eight o'clock in the morning.... We watched them out the window, and they walked along the street to come to this place, and the formidable array of cops and firemen scared them off.

Still, we did have a lot of marchers. [Arshile] Gorky had a great big thing made out of pressed wood. It was a huge, heavy thing—you know, like a certain kind of flat, Cubist sculpture that was in vogue in those days. When they tried to get it out [of the Action Committee's headquarters], of course, it was too big. They took the window out in the back and so forth, and they finally had to take it all apart and put it back together again out in the street. It took four men to carry it. I remember that one of them was Byron Browne.... He was a big, strong guy, and I remember him because you could always see him. He had blonde hair blowing in the wind, and he was taller than anybody else. The parade was like one of these Italian fêtes that you see where they carry huge religious things; forty or fifty people carry them down the street and bounce them up and down....

I'd forgotten all about that—thank God. You know, there were so damn many things going on. You just can't keep all that crap in your head. The only reason it [the parade] went on was because nobody had anything else to do, and the fact that people were able to do something in concert was very important.... It was a...needed social thing to get the artists who were literally in the gutter into some kind of coordinated action. It... had nothing to do with Communism, even though Communists were active [in the effort]. They… had this habit of organizing people on some level where it had a common denominator of interest for them. When the government set up the art projects, here was a common employer, you know, and there was something to talk about to a lot of people because they had a common objective and economic problems, all valuable and authentic. So we had good reason.

Stuart Davis

FEDERAL WORKS AGENCY
NEW YORK CITY WPA WAR SERVICES
ART SERVICES

PASS

Signature *Burgoyne Diller*

To Sections

All

Issued by

Oscar H. Julius

Work Project Superintendent

SU4

Burgoyne Diller

1906 – 1965

While painter Burgoyne Diller was one of the first American
exponents of the art of Piet Mondrian, it could be argued
that his greatest influence was not as a painter, but as head
of the mural division in the New York City section of the
Federal Art Project. In this excerpt from an interview conducted
by Harlan Phillips in 1964, Diller talks about the camaraderie
among artists during the Depression. The interview was
part of a special project funded by the Ford Foundation to
document New Deal art programs. Later Diller describes
the beginnings of the WPA in New York and the chicken-and-
egg problem of how to put artists to work on murals that were
not yet commissioned.

Burgoyne Diller's "pass" for the Federal Works Agency New York City WPA War Services, ca. 1935.
Kenneth and Emma-Stina Prescott research material on artists, 1930–1987.

Burgoyne Diller: As a matter of fact there's something that's unforgettable about that period. There was a wonderful sense of belonging to something, even if it was an underprivileged and downhearted time. You just weren't a stranger. Now we've reverted back again to the days when artists rarely meet. If they do, it's under such artificial circumstances, and they're so infested with hangers-on, and it becomes, you know, a battle of clichés. Everything else in the world except the very vital, fundamental issues that you were confronted with then that made you sleep together [i.e. become strange bedfellows].

Harlan Phillips: A complete change.

Because then it was a matter of survival, but, as I say, it was exciting. I cannot look back on it and say, "Here, this was a time of pain." God knows, there were problems, there was unhappiness, there were many

things. . . . We were all aware of it. The differences between ourselves aesthetically—well, they degenerated into a kind of quibble unless they were being utilized for political reasons. In other words, you could be a very academic painter. I could be a very abstract painter. We could get along fine. The only time we had a pitched battle was if you decided that painting had to be directed only toward the Marxian function of propaganda, or something of the sort, and I had the unholy attitude of art for art's sake, you know. Then of course we'd become terribly involved. This is what happened in the Artists' Union, the Artists' Congress, those organizations, but as I said, there was such a basic thing to hold them that no matter how much they would quarrel with each other, they still had to hold together, or else they'd be lost. . .

Yes. Well, is there an ingredient in this coming together, the fact that they had a common employer, the government? How did they look upon that?

I think that the coming together started before the government stepped in, because I still remember hanging paintings on the fence in Washington Square when men like Vernon Porter and some others organized and got the city's permission for the artists to sell works in Washington Square. [In 1932 painter Vernon Carroll Porter organized the Washington Square Outdoor Art Show. Conceived as an annual spring and fall sales exhibition to help artists survive the Depression, it continues in some form today.] Now that was the beginning of these Washington Square shows, but believe me, at that time you had all the name artists hanging their wares in Washington Square and hoping against hope, you know, that they'd sell anything for anything, any price. . . . And, as I said, there [in the Washington Square shows] you had the beginning of a kind of cooperative spirit and the necessity for cooperation before your projects came into existence.

◀ ◀ ◀

Apparently, New York City had been voted . . . or, rather, granted a certain amount of money. A certain budgetary limitation was set up, but the funds would become available. Now understand, this means money to be spent. Therefore, you had to have people working to earn that money, and this comes to putting people to work. . . . But we had a double-fold responsibility. You couldn't put people to work on nothing. The only thing you could do immediately was to say, "Well here, try experimenting with some mural ideas," if you felt the man was capable of this work. You see, your work was submitted to a committee, and it was decided whether you could be an easel painter. Now that was easy. We all could paint, you see. Or to a sculptor, you know: "Go off and prepare some sketches for a sculpture." You could put them to work immediately, but in a division like the mural division or architectural sculpture, it was a different thing, because we had to get the sponsorship of public institutions in order to assign anything. Those people we felt were more immediately able to start developing projects we assigned to just general thinking about the things, about the mural, because don't forget, very few men had had the opportunity of working on walls. We felt that if they just exercised a little bit until we could find them a sponsor, you see, why we'd be that much up on the game. I know that in my case it was a question of spending half the day, you know, on the committee, accepting the artists, enrolling them and

Burgoyne Diller

assigning them to what I thought was reasonable that would help in the total picture that was developing. Then the other half or more of your time was spent in going out to city agencies and talking with people in public libraries and so on and having them request a mural. Now the commitment at the time on their part was really that they would have the mural. They could order a mural through the head of the department, through their agency.... If they were a grade school or a high school, or whatever, you'd have to go through the Board of Education and have the Board of Education make the request. But the original request came from the school itself. So we'd have to talk to the school principals and so on and say, "Well, here, we've looked at your building, and we think there's an opportunity of having a mural in the auditorium, or in the hallways or something."... If they were interested, why we'd develop it from there. As fast as we could get these institutions committed to sponsorship, we could assign artists to make tentative sketches for the job.... We had to have men at work in order to use the money that had been designated for the area and for the activity.... So it was an impossible sort of task, but one that you thought you had to do something about. . . . There were plenty of available spaces. Now I don't mean it was easy to convince these people that they should have a mural, or whatever, I mean, some of them of course wanted to have hearing after hearing to discuss it, and then they'd have to cover themselves. They had within their own family, you know, they'd have their Art Chairman and some of the other people in the school, you know, go into lengthy debates about the subject matter and so on and so on. By the time we got the sponsorship sometimes there could be quite a delay. This meant that you had to hit five places to make sure you'd have one next week to assign to an artist. Then as fast as you could assign the artists, then you could assign the assistant, start assigning assistants, probably one first just to help the artist gather data. Most of the murals involved subject matter that needed research and so on. They could start doing research, and whatever, and then a little later, why you might assign more if it were a large job, you know, because then you have the actual job of setting up big wall space. . . . Most of the [school] principals were cooperative; not only cooperative, but some went to great lengths to aid in the research because in some subjects it was rather difficult. They asked some of their teachers, you know, specialists who'd be more specialized in fields, to assist and so on. On the whole, the sponsors were really quite cooperative, but you see these—the majority, as I said—but this isn't the kind of thing that makes news.

It's always the—

The thing that makes news is the one who uncovered the fact that a mural being done in the music room of this high school was done by a young woman who had worked on a mural with Diego Rivera, and when they found that out, that, as far as they were concerned, made her a Communist. It was a fresco. It was half-finished, and it was torn down by orders of the principal. [Diller is referring to Lucienne Bloch's mural *The Evolution of Music* in the George Washington High School, New York City, 1937–38.] Now he had no authority to do this because he should have gone to the New York City Art Commission, and it should have gone back through the process, because in the mural itself, the girl had taken ancient musical instruments and painted a frieze around the music room. Even then no one claimed that there was one iota of leftist or any other kind of commentary, or any kind of commentary. No charge was made like that at all, but he had found out through "a good soul" that this girl had worked on a mural with Diego Rivera. What her political viewpoints were, I have no idea. All I know is she was doing a job for us, and there wasn't one iota of anything there that the most reactionary person could possibly protest as far as the motif of the thing, or the coloring, or anything at all. These are the things that you read about. We had 125 going on at one time, but you read about this on the front page, but not of the other 124. You know it was very unfair.

Burgoyne Diller

Dorothea Lange
1895–1965

In 1964 and 1965, art historian Richard K. Doud interviewed
photographers and administrators who worked on the Farm
Security Administration (FSA), a New Deal project designed to
assist poor farmers during the Depression. From 1935 to 1945,
the FSA employed photographers such as Irene Delano, Walker
Evans, Theodore Jung, Dorothea Lange, Russell Lee, Carl Mydans,
Gordon Parks, Edwin and Louise Rosskam, Arthur Rothstein,
Ben Shahn, and Marion Post Wolcott to document rural poverty
in the United States. The FSA photographs, especially those
illustrating the desperate conditions in the Dust Bowl and
displaced farmers migrating West in search of work, are some
of the most famous images in the history of photography.

In his unique series of interviews, Doud questioned the
photographers about their work for the FSA. In this segment
from a 1964 interview, Dorothea Lange describes what it was
like working for the FSA and the moment that she became a
"social observer."

Richard K. Doud: On your first trip to Washington, D.C., when you were introduced to the people who were going to document rural poverty and perhaps discussed what was to be done and how it was going to be done, what were your reactions to the whole thing?... How did you feel about the actual organization of the assignment, being part of the Farm Security or Resettlement Administration at the time; working for a man [Roy Stryker, who directed the FSA's photo-documentary project] who wasn't a photographer but rather was an economics professor working in conjunction with other photographers whom you might or might not have known or heard of?

Dorothea Lange: You speak of organization; I didn't find any. You speak of work plans; I didn't find any. I didn't find an economics professor. I didn't find any of those things. It was a hot, muggy early summer, and I found a little office, tucked away, where nobody knew exactly what he was going to do or how to do it. And this is no criticism, because you walked into an atmosphere of a very special kind of freedom; anyone who tells you anything else and dresses us up in official light is not truthful, because it wasn't that way. That freedom—you found your own way without criticism from anyone— was special and germane to the project. Roy Stryker was... not organized, but he had a very hospitable mind. He had an instinct for what's important. And he was a *colossal watchdog* for his people.

I want to hear more about the work you eventually did in the field. I've always been intrigued by the fact that you people could go to a part of the country that you'd never seen before, that you knew nothing (or very little) about, and could do such a sensitive, all-encompassing job of photographing it. I'd like to know a number of things. First, how did you approach a specific assignment? Once you were there—I know this is hard to put into words—how did you decide what to photograph? You couldn't take pictures of everything, of every person. Yet it seems that each of you had a knack of always photographing the right things. Was there a secret formula there, or was it instinct, as you mentioned before?

Well, you've put your finger on the heart of the Farm Security Administration venture. Because it's almost inexplicable, that particular—you know, there is a word for it: élan. I would understand it better myself if it applied to one of us only. But it didn't. It caught… like it was contagious. When you went into that office,…you were so welcome, they were so glad to see you. Did you have a good trip? Was everything all right? What you were doing was important. *You* were important.…Which made you feel that you had a responsibility. Not to those people in the office, but in general. A person expands when he has an important thing to do. You felt it. In the field, you were almost always alone, turned loose, unknown, very often unprepared, against a background where something was expected of you. You found your way, but never the way big-shot photographers did, not like the big-magazine boys do it now. We found our way in, slid in on the edges. We trusted our hunches, we lived; it was hard, hard living. In fact, it was rather rough, living not too far from the people we were working with. We ate better food, slept in better beds, and so on; we weren't deprived, really.

But you didn't ever quit in the middle of something because it was uncomfortable. And with the actual people, you worked with a certain common denominator. Now, if they asked who you were and they heard you were a government representative interested in their difficulties or condition, that's very different from going in and saying, "I'm working for *Look* magazine, which wants to take pictures of you."…We were not spotlighting, but were more unobtrusive. We photographers were somewhat picked at random; we weren't hand-picked. We were educated on the job. The government gave us a magnificent education, every one of us. And I don't know of [any FSA photographer who has] fallen by the wayside, do you?

◀ ◀ ◀

I'd like to ask you to recall just one or two really memorable experiences, or the first thing perhaps that comes to mind when you think

Dorothea Lange

There are so many levels on which I could answer that. I think often, with some satisfaction, of a weekend in April of 1934 or '35. I went down to Imperial Valley, California, to photograph the harvesting of one of the crops: early peas or carrots. The assignment was [to document] the beginning of the migration, as the workers started there in the beginning of the season and then as they moved [north]. I was going to follow them along. I had completed what I had to do, and I started for home, driving up the main highway, which ran the length of the state. It was a very rainy afternoon. I stopped to get gas, and there was a car full of people, a white American family, at the gas station. They looked very woebegone to me. The license plate on their car said "Oklahoma."

I got out of my car and asked them about which way they were going, whether they were looking for work.… They said, "We've been blown out." I asked what they meant, and then they told me about the dust storm, how they had gotten up that morning and saw that they had no crop, [knew that] they had to get out, and left. They drove all of that day, maybe two hundred miles—no, three or four hundred miles. The story of migratory labor in California is an old one. But I saw *these* people. And I couldn't wait. I photographed [what was happening]. I [documented] those first ones. That was…the first day of the landslide that cut this continent, and it's still going on. I don't mean that people haven't migrated before, but this shaking off of people from their roots started with those big storms. It was like a movement of the earth, you see. And that rainy afternoon I remember, because I made the discovery. It was unobserved up to that time. There are books and books and books on that subject now.

This was the American exodus?

Yes. It's still going on today. The war came, and of course set off another big jolt, like an earthquake. But I went home that day a discoverer, a real social observer. Luckily, my eyes were open to it. I could have been like all the other people on that highway and not seen it. We don't see what is right before us. We don't see it 'till someone tells us. But this I discovered myself. This thing they call social erosion. I saw it. That was a day.

Dorothea Lange

A. Hyatt Mayor

1901–1980

A. Hyatt Mayor had a distinguished career as an art historian,   **45**
author, and curator of prints at the Metropolitan Museum of
Art, New York. In his final years, he was also an active member
of the Archives of American Art Advisory Committee, enlivening
its twice-yearly deliberations with his particular blend of
enthusiasm and wit.

In this excerpt from an interview conducted by Paul
Cummings in 1969, Mayor recalls how he "stumbled into" his
job at the Metropolitan Museum, describes working with the
legendary print curator William Ivins, and discusses the early
development of the museum's collection.

A. Hyatt Mayor: . . . When I wanted to get married, of course, it was in the draggy depths of the Depression. So I hawked myself around to all the people I knew in the universities on the eastern seaboard, who would just have none of me. It was just "throw that man out, it breaks my heart." And finally, just completely by accident, I stumbled into the Print Department of the Metropolitan Museum. Then [William] Ivins had the *courage* to hire me. And, believe me, it took courage, because I had no qualifications whatsoever beyond being able to read the languages. And that was his reason, that I could inform myself, I could teach myself. . . .

Paul Cummings: So what were you hired to do at the Metropolitan?

I was hired to learn the Print Department business. And I was hired because I had not gone to the Fogg [Art Museum, Harvard University] and was, therefore, not warped, tainted, smeared, or whatever. Ivins was anti-Fogg, although he was a great friend of Paul J. Sachs [associate director, Fogg Art Museum]. In a sense he was right. Because the Fogg in those days did not turn out museum curators; it turned out directors. . . . Back in the '20s, museums were springing up all over the country and what they needed was bright personable young men who could persuade people to give money, keep the old ladies happy, and get things going. And they didn't have to know much. But they had to know something of the world of dealers and a smattering of works of art. But that was not what Ivins wanted for *his* assistant. I was simply turned loose with no instructions except that I was to learn the collection. . . .

I've been able to find out very, very little about Ivins.

Oh, really?

I'm quite curious about how he worked and what kind of personality he had and all this sort of thing.

Well, he was a very tall, slatternly kind of man; he didn't quite shamble like the two halves of two camels the way [Edward] Steichen does, but he walked a little like that. And he looked like a sort of [Johann

Wolfgang von] Goethe, rather consciously sloppy. He had the Harvard hat, all in holes and tatters; but that wasn't because it was an old hat. That was style, it was quite deliberately conscious. He would come into the museum at eleven o'clock in the morning; he was more an owl than a lark, and he'd work late at night as lawyers do. As a lawyer [Ivins had a law degree], he had an intemperate way of arguing; it was always the *argumentum ad hominem*.... He had a terrible temper, an absolutely ungovernable, mad temper. And when a fit came on him, he simply was a being who should be put away and not seen until he cooled off, radioactive for the moment, you see.... I would have flounced out certainly if I had been a bachelor. There's no question about that. If I hadn't had school bills and pediatricians and diapers to pay for, I would not have lasted. But somehow to pay for a family gives one a stomach for crow, and it would have been a great mistake to have left.

◀ ◀ ◀

I'm curious about the early collections or groups of prints that came into the department. There was the first [major gift], the Harris B. Dick collection. Were there other ones like that?

Yes. There were a good many. A charming little old lady . . . Georgiana Sargent . . . had an Albrecht Dürer woodcut of Samson and the Lions, made around 1500, a very early one. This was part of her father's collection. Her father collected biblical subjects. And she said, "This is so fresh and new. Of course I'm sure it is a facsimile but you might want it perhaps." Ivins looked at it very, very closely indeed and said, "No, my dear, it's not a facsimile. It's just simply about the best impression that's survived from this block." She was delighted with that and gave her father's whole collection. . . . Then Junius Morgan, who I think was the nephew of J. P. Morgan, was very much interested in Dürer. He sat in Paris for some thirty years collecting Dürer prints and other things, too. He would swap out things when he got better impressions, so he was always bettering what he had. Finally, he sold his copper plates

A. Hyatt Mayor

to the museum and gave us his woodcuts. Which is a wonderful thing. That was in the early '20s, I don't quite remember. So that gave us the best Dürer collection in the country, or, as a matter of fact, one of the best Dürer collections anywhere.

Then perhaps one of the most remarkable gifts came from Felix Warburg, who lived in the [mansion that the] Jewish Museum occupies now. On the billiard table in the billiard room (it was the corner room on the ground floor), were large portfolios . . . of prints. . . . Gerald Warburg told me that he and his brothers were very annoyed by this collection because, whenever they wanted to shoot pool, they had to [remove] these great big heavy volumes. . . . When [Felix Warburg] died, he bequeathed his collection to Mrs. Warburg; . . . at her death, the children were to take what they wanted . . . and the remainder was to come to the Metropolitan. Well, the family got together and said they didn't want any of it, and that they would like the Metropolitan to choose immediately (this was in 1941) what it either lacked altogether or had in worse impressions. A very good proviso, you see. In other words, we were not to take duplicates; we would only swap. Absolutely correct.... It was a big collection, three or four hundred things, so the whole batch of us worked very hard on this and very scrupulously observed the [Warburgs'] requests. And in came some of the most wonderful Rembrandts you *ever*, ever saw! Oh, my God, things you'd never, never get nowadays or again. Never. And the wonderful early German things that had belonged to Junius Morgan! Because Morgan had bought the early Germans. And all sorts of things. It was one of the very, very great gifts. Then Mrs. Havemeyer's collection, which came in 1929, I think it was, also contained some wonderful things:... beautiful impressions of the color etchings by her friend Mary Cassatt, as well as marvelous Rembrandts and some Dürers.

You must have quite a large Rembrandt collection?

Yes. Ivins was extremely sensible there. He never bought what people collected because he knew that [these prints] would be dropped in the poor man's hat someday. He was right.... And that was very intelligent of him, very. He never bought Whistlers because they would come in. And they did.

A. Hyatt Mayor

Edith Gregor Halpert

1900–1970

In 1926, at age twenty-six, Edith Gregor Halpert opened
one of the first art galleries in Greenwich Village. She was
extraordinary for her time, considering that few women
pursued careers and that she was completely devoted to
the fledgling field of American art. In her forty-four years in
the business, Halpert developed new sales strategies, cultivated
collectors, and aggressively promoted the artists she believed
in— Stuart Davis, Yasuo Kuniyoshi, Jacob Lawrence, John
Marin, Charles Sheeler, and others. She also created a market
for American folk art, which she believed to be the indigenous
root of American modernism.

Among other things, Halpert learned that colorful
anecdotes sell art. In 1962 and 1963, when she was interviewed
for the Archives of American Art by Harlan B. Phillips, she
revealed herself to be a seasoned raconteur. In the resulting
819-page transcript, Halpert embellished her recollections
with lively stories—some true, others invented. In this segment,
she talks about her vision for a different kind of art gallery.

Edith Gregor Halpert, ca. 1920. Photographer unknown. Downtown Gallery records, 1824 –1974.

Edith Gregor Halpert: Well, the whole idea was to make the gallery an intimate thing. In those days, a man like "Pop" Hart, who walked into Knoedler's [Gallery, New York City] holding a banana and was kicked out, would not be [welcome in any other gallery but mine]. As a kid, I was not admitted to any of the galleries. . . . They practically told you to get the hell out, except Montross [Gallery], but they were very, very few.

Everything you do is a result of something that happened before, so I wanted to make this gallery welcoming, which is why I called it "Our Gallery," so that anybody could come in at any time, day and evening, and so on. Then I decided that I didn't like that name. After a while, [the sculptor William] Zorach came in. I said, "I've got to change the name of the gallery." He said, "Why don't you change the name to Downtown Gallery?" I couldn't think of anything more divine than that.

It was the only gallery downtown, and it's strange that there's this big revival after thirty-five years—you know, they have suddenly discovered that the Village is a [good] place for a gallery. "Our Gallery" didn't last long. It lasted until I used up all the stationery I had. When only ten sheets of stationery were left, I changed the name. In the Village, anything went. . . . I made the gallery very uptownish through my attire, but very downtownish in the whole idea of having people meet, having collectors see the artists—that was terribly important. . . . There's one wonderful story. . . . First, I have to get us a drink.

A very early client was Edith Wetmore of Newport, Rhode Island. Her father [George P. Wetmore] was governor of Rhode Island, and later a U.S. senator. She and her sister Maud were raised by a German governess, and they both talked with a very strong German accent. Well, she came down to the gallery in about 1928—I don't think it was the first year, maybe the second. Everybody was talking about the gallery, which I conceived as an early American setting: "There's something absolutely fantastic! There's an art gallery in the Village, and a young woman is running it, and you see early American objects, hooked rugs, early American furniture." Well, I showed Edith Wetmore a painting. She said, "I'd like to see it in daylight." The entrance was three steps down from the sidewalk. It was a brownstone like all the speakeasies, so it was dim. I had electric light, but Edith Wetmore insisted on seeing the picture in daylight, so I took it outside, and I leaned it against something. I don't think she bought that picture, and I remember the very strange look of amusement on her face. But she did buy something that day. About a week later, she came down in an open car—what did they call them in those days, roasters?— with two young men from—I don't know whether they were nephews, or what—but they were wearing—what were those fur coats called?

53

Harlan B. Phillips: Raccoon coats.

Yes. Well, she brought them swinging into the gallery and said, "This is the gallery where they show pictures leaning against garbage cans." Many of these people would come in for the full treatment—you know, the full Left Bank touch. . . . [A. Conger] Goodyear, Mrs. Rockefeller. Richard De Wolfe. They all had boxes at the opera and, if they weren't going, they would send me tickets. It was always *La Bohème.* One whisper of that opera now can make me scream, because I saw it about eight times! Finally, I returned the tickets and said, "Please!" But my relationship with these people was completely along those lines.

. . . Seymour Knox of the Albright Gallery [later the Albright-Knox Gallery, Buffalo, New York] came down with the museum's director at that time (it might have been [Andrew C.] Ritchie), who told him to come to the gallery and look at the work of Yasuo Kuniyoshi. I was so eager to make this sale, I said, "Oh, Mr. Knox, I will take you to Mr. Kuniyoshi's studio." Yash's studio was on 14th Street, in that famous building right above an underwear shop, and you had to go through the shop to get into the building.

Mr. Knox thought that 14th Street was fascinating! All these little girls walking around in short skirts, and all those cheap stores — you know, dress shops charging $3.98 for a dress, and the underwear shop. I said, "This is where we go in." We went through the shop to the hallway, and he was absolutely petrified. He kept looking at me, "Where are you taking me?" It was an artists' studio building, very inexpensive. We had to walk up four flights of stairs. There were garbage cans on each landing. We got to Yash's door. Of course, he had no telephone [so he wasn't expecting guests]. Who had a telephone then in a studio? A very pretty girl came out, and Knox looked. We went in. Knox saw a picture and bought it for the Albright Gallery. Coming out, he was so excited, he said, "Mrs. Halpert, this is *La Bohème!*"

This was really the attitude. It was what attracted many of the uptowners. Believe me, there were no downtowners buying art! I don't think I had anybody with less than a couple of million bucks who bought anything. . . .

◀ ◀ ◀

[The Parisian art dealer Ambroise] Vollard told me how to peddle art. It was absolutely wonderful, and I remember every word he said to me. My French wasn't very good, but I understood everything.

"Never own more than fifty percent and never invest a nickel." It was the most beautiful hunk of advice. He started this with Gauguin. He bought Gauguins and sold fifty percent of them for the full investment, and then he sat on his fifty percent until he sold it to ten dealers to distribute. The dealers would invest the money and would knock themselves out to put this guy [Gauguin] on the map. Vollard waited until Gauguin's art was so expensive that the fifty percent was worth about five thousand percent. That is a philosophy of merchandising that I haven't followed. It was too easy. It certainly was not good for the artist. French artists were happy about it, but American artists won't take it. The dealer remains the villain, and the artist is the poor little helpless soul the dealer takes advantage of. Yeah! I need musical accompaniment for that—wow! Every time I see a play or read a book about artists, I just burn up—good God! I'm still waiting after thirty-six years for the time I can take advantage of an artist. In my experience, there are only two artists who have been honorable, two artists who haven't taken advantage of me: Stuart Davis and Charles Sheeler.

Edith Gregor Halpert

Jacob Lawrence

1917–2000

Painter Jacob Lawrence was just twenty-four when his
Migration *series made him nationally famous. The series—*
sixty narrative panels portraying the movement of African
Americans from the rural South to the urban North after
World War I—was exhibited in 1941 at Edith Halpert's
Downtown Gallery in New York City. Moreover, twenty-six
were published in Fortune *magazine in the same year, at*
a time when few African American artists were given any
visibility in the predominantly white American art world.

In this excerpt from an interview conducted by Carroll
Greene in 1968 for the Archives of American Art, Lawrence
talks about his early exposure to art in an after-school program
at a settlement house in Harlem, the concepts underlying his
Migration *series, and the strong influence of Josef Albers on*
his work and his teaching.

Jacob Lawrence, 1957. Photograph by Alfredo Valente. Alfredo Valente papers, 1941–1978.

Jacob Lawrence: I spent the years between the ages of twelve and, say, seventeen, eighteen in the upper 130s and 140s in New York City.

Carroll Greene: Were you near Striver's Row [a popular epithet for the area of West 138th and West 139th Streets between Powell and Douglass Boulevards in Harlem, so-called in the 1920s and 1930s because affluent African Americans lived there] ?

Yes. Right off Seventh Avenue...

What was your attitude toward Striver's Row?

At that time, I didn't have any attitude. You see, my interests were so involved in art, but not in a scholarly manner. Because I didn't know what art was in that way. It was something I just liked to do, like some kids ride bikes and some kids hike, some kids join the Boy Scouts. I never even thought of being a professional artist at that time. I didn't even know what that meant. It was beyond my experience. I didn't see an art gallery until I was about eighteen years of age. Which is very unusual for kids who have... art in their homes, and that type of background. Art was something I liked to do. I liked to color. And that was it. This was my exposure. At the settlement house [an after-school program at Utopia Children's House in Harlem], I was exposed to arts and crafts: soap carving, leatherwork, woodwork, and painting. It was an arts-and-crafts thing. I went into painting, working with poster paints and things of that sort. That was my first real exposure.

◀ ◀ ◀

Tell us a little bit about your series depicting the migration of the Negro. What were you trying to do there?

Many of the things you do early on you don't realize all that they mean, and sometimes you add other dimensions of meaning to them later. . . . The Migration was a great epic drama. The Negro has been the focal point of this drama. We understand ourselves as Americans in part through the Negro experience. So you select such a subject if you are interested in man and his desire to always better himself. You cannot pick a better symbol in America to point this up than the

Negro experience and the Migration. And of course the Migration brings up all sorts of social implications. The school situation, which we talk about today; the poverty; the people who were successful—I don't want to dwell only on the negative aspects—people moving and getting a better education. Out of this, we have the children of today who are making a contribution in various areas. It was their parents who took part in this Migration, came up, worked, and so on. These are all things I was trying to say in this series, as I look back in retrospect.

In the series, there are twenty-six scenes in tempera on board.

Well, there are sixty altogether. Twenty-six were reproduced in *Fortune* magazine, you see.

Where are they?

Fortunately, they have been kept together. The Museum of Modern Art in New York owns half.

Given by Mrs. David Levy.

That's right. And the Phillips Memorial Gallery in Washington has the other half. My *Migration* series was exhibited at the Downtown Gallery. That's how *Fortune* happened to feature it. So I will always owe Edith Halpert, really—I think she is one of the great American dealers. She was one of the first to really become involved with young American artists. You see, prior to that time, the dealers were involved mostly with Europeans, or with Americans who had gone to Europe and then come back. She was a real pioneer....

◀ ◀ ◀

Since about 1940 I've been a professional artist. That is, in the sense of making a living from my art and as a teacher. By the way, you asked me who are some of the major influences on my work—I forgot to mention one, because I have a tendency to think in terms of content rather than form. There is a man whom I think very few people... would associate me with him—and that is Josef Albers.

Albers!

Jacob Lawrence

Yes. Like Edith Halpert, who had a great influence on me in a commercial professional sense, he had a great influence on me in a plastic, aesthetic sense. Years ago [1946] he invited me down to Black Mountain College, in Black Mountain, North Carolina, for the summer as a guest instructor. And there I had the experience of coming into contact with one of the great teachers of our time. I heard his lectures and that type of thing. As I said before, this may seem strange because if you look at our works there's no apparent connection; he's handling purely abstract shapes, not even forms, but shapes, and not involved in content as I am, you see. So his work seems so far removed from mine. But yet I would say that much of my teaching is based on that of the Bauhaus and Josef Albers, who was part of the Bauhaus. And my approach to teaching is based on that philosophy.

Would you care to elaborate on your interpretation of this philosophy, how you yourself have adapted it to your own approach to teaching?

The Bauhaus? Yes. Well, I try to get the student to appreciate form and shape, line, color, texture, and space, regardless of what the content may be. The content can be abstract or it can be figurative. But I try to get the student to appreciate this because, when the student does, then he can almost do anything (this, by the way, was the Bauhaus theory). . . . I try to point out that there's less chance of your becoming just illustrative when you become involved with the plastic elements of painting. So in short this is how I try to adapt Bauhaus ideas to teaching. You don't see a head as a head, but you see it as a form and as a shape. And you can work as realistically as you care to. But if you just see things as they are, the chances are that you will become more illustrative and you will never develop from this, you know, move away from this. The other way, you become much more plastic, much more aesthetic in what you're doing.

So much of your painting since the *Migration* series has centered around Negro, or as is popular today, black subject matter. Would you care to comment on that?

Yes. I think this is a natural thing. My beginnings, as with most Negroes in the United States, are rooted in the Negro experience. All I knew at one time was the Negro experience. My whole background: Negro family, Negro community, everything was Negro. So I think it was natural that I would use this symbol for my expression, you see. I think this is very important to what we're saying here. Several years ago, I started an American history series that does not pertain strictly to the Negro theme [*Struggle… From the History of the American People,* 1955–56; thirty panels, dispersed]. But I think my reason for doing it had something to do with the Negro consciousness: in doing it, I wanted to show how and to what degree the Negro had participated in American history. If you go through the [*Struggle*] paintings, there are very few Negroes in them. I purposefully included Negroes in my depiction of George Washington crossing the Delaware because I wanted to show how the Negro has been such a natural part of the American experience. So the one time I did move away from my subject, my own Negro experience, both historically and personally, remained a factor.

This experience as a Negro in the United States, has it made you different from other American artists, or do you think it has added another dimension?

It's added a different dimension. Naturally, I can't speak for all Negro artists, and I would even venture to say for most Negro artists. I couldn't make an absolute statement, but I would definitely say that I think any experience that evolves because of your ethnic background, and especially pertaining to the Negro, is a special kind of experience. It has definitely added to my work a different kind of dimension than, say, the work of another artist would have. And since we as a people have not been integrated (we may never be)—because of the physical difference, you know—that doesn't mean that it'll always be a negative thing, but it cannot help but influence my thinking and my work and my whole being. I wouldn't say that it has added a deeper dimension, but I will say definitely another kind of dimension than other artists who may not have had the same kind of experience I've had of being Negro.

Jacob Lawrence

Emmy Lou Packard

1914–1998

In the late 1920s, Emmy Lou Packard lived with her family in Mexico City, where she became acquainted with Diego Rivera. In 1940 she studied fresco and sculpture at the California School of Fine Arts, San Francisco. That year, she worked as an assistant to Rivera on his fresco for the 1939–40 Golden Gate International Exposition on Treasure Island, in the middle of San Francisco Bay. The fresco, Marriage of the Artistic Expression of the North and of the South on This Continent, *also known as* Pan-American Unity, *is now at the City College of San Francisco. After the project, Packard returned to Mexico with Rivera and his wife, Frida Kahlo, and spent a year living with them.*

In an interview conducted by Mary McChesney in 1964, Packard talks about working with Rivera and other assistants on the Pan-American Unity *fresco.*

Diego Rivera & Emmy Lou Packard working on the fresco *Pan-American Unity*, on Treasure Island, San Francisco Bay, 1940. Photograph by Gabriel Moulin. Emmy Lou Packard papers, 1900–1999.

Emmy Lou Packard: Things around Rivera, no matter where he was, were always boiling. He attracted people partly because of his reputation, of course, and many wanted to see him or work with him. So there was a great deal of rivalry, and we had to keep people away. In fact, a guard was stationed to prevent people from going to the studio and up on the scaffold. Tim Pflueger [an architect and one of the organizers of the 1939–40 Golden Gate International Exposition in San Francisco] would often bring important people up to, you know, put a brushstroke on the mural. Rivera was fairly patient with this, but I remember one evening they kept him talking a little too long, so that when they left and he tried the plaster, he found it had dried too much. He had one of his infrequent tantrums (Frida called them "coráges") and simply tore the plaster with the back of the fresco brush (a big heavy brush) and ripped it up. When he got extremely angry, he always swore in French....

In general, Rivera tried pretty hard, under extremely difficult conditions that were to some extent self-imposed. He had this enormous job to do in a short time and was a prodigious worker anyway, so we would often be there on the fresco—he would have enough plaster spread so that we'd be there anywhere from eighteen to twenty-four hours, sometimes thirty, while he was working steadily, and we often left at dawn, because he had worked straight through the night, not wanting to lose the wet plaster as long as he could keep at it. . . .

[Arthur] Niendorff did some of the technical jobs, such as painting the Shell Building or the Ford motor in the mural, things that were purely technical, such as looking up, or getting a photograph of a Ford motor and simply rendering this exactly as it was in the fresco. This kind of job didn't interest Rivera, and Niendorff did it very well, so he would often do these very detailed things. I remember the first day on the job, Rivera was way up in the top left-hand corner painting the image of the ancient Aztec civilization, and he assigned to me a little square courtyard, saying, "Now when you were a child in Mexico, you went out to the open air school and you remember that they had courtyards? You remember you were in some of those courtyards? Now, it's up to you, if you're ever going to be a mural painter, you have to cultivate memory. The thing that is absolutely necessary for a mural painter is a tremendous memory." "So," he said, "you sit there and you remember what was in that courtyard and you put it down there. I'm not going to help you a bit." I tried very hard, and he was satisfied with the result, thank goodness. It was a tremendous feat for me.

> **Mary McChesney:** How large a section was the courtyard, how large a piece of the mural did it cover?

Oh, this was just very, very small, probably not more than six inches. This was just a small part of an enormous area. However, he required every small thing you did to be proper. I remember a little while later—let's see, it was a matter of a knot in a rope—he asked me to paint the knot in a rope. I painted it, and he was very cross. He said, "You've never looked at a knot in a rope."… He made me take it all out. He took off the plaster. He said, "Go tie a knot and look at it and draw it." Which I did. These details were very important to him. They had to be right.

One very amusing thing happened when the mural was almost finished. Of course, thousands of people came to see the mural every day, and one man pointed out that the flag on Treasure Island, which Rivera had drawn, was obviously blowing in a direction that the winds practically never blew in San Francisco. The fog was blowing in one direction and the flag was blowing in the other direction. Diego loved to have this kind of criticism…

> Did he change the direction of the flag?

No, he didn't because it would have meant taking out plaster and he was far beyond that point. It would have meant actually moving the scaffold by that time.

◀ ◀ ◀

At the beginning of each day's work, a new, final coat of plaster

Emmy Lou Packard

Yes. [Matt] Barnes and Niendorff would put on the plaster, which had
to be very carefully troweled until it made a smooth painting surface.
By the way, on that mural Rivera employed a technique that he had not
used before. The upper parts, which would be farther from the viewer's
eye, were both plastered and painted in a rougher manner than the
lower parts, which would be closer to the viewer. There, the plaster was
smoother in finish and the painting somewhat more detailed.

As Rivera would not usually get to work before noon, since he didn't go to
sleep before dawn, the plastering was timed so it would be ready to paint
at 1:00 p.m. A plasterer would phone Rivera from Treasure Island and tell
him everything was nearly ready. Rivera would arrive just as the plaster
was at the right stage. The plaster can't be too wet, or it begins to mix
with the paint and the brush will disturb its surface. If the plaster is too
dry, the color (powdered pigments mixed with water) will not sink into
the surface. It has to be just at a point where the plaster is still damp, the
color will sink into it, and then a very, very tiny coat of calcium carbon-
ate, which is limestone really, will form on the surface. This is true fresco.
And this surface is very beautiful, a translucent color. . . .

◄ ◄ ◄

Well, it varied, but Rivera would sometimes do, let's see, oh, twenty-five
or thirty square feet, less if the design was complex and detailed. His
method was to underpaint in black. Of course, white pigment is not
used in fresco: white is the surface of the plaster. So he underpainted
in vine black, establishing the dark and light tones under the final
coat of transparent color. I have the whole list of colors he used on the
City College fresco. Mainly Weber Dry Colors; they were ground by an
assistant on a marble slab. They couldn't be too finely or too coarsely
ground. The black and white was simply to establish the tonal values,

and then the color, the transparent color was washed over. I believe the method was used in Italian Renaissance fresco painting, and I believe this is why he did it in this way. It did give a very beautiful, deep transparency to the finished painting.

As his assistant, what were your responsibilities?

I simply painted whatever Diego ordered me to. I did some of the underpainting. Most of the areas I did were fairly straightforward, although as I gained experience, he gave me more difficult things to do. As I stated earlier, I painted San Francisco Bay, which is quite a large area in the mural. After he had established the manner of painting the bay, he then simply turned the rest of it over to me so that, whenever an area of bay was needed, I painted it in. It was done in alternate strokes of ultramarine and, I believe, cobalt: a green-blue and a purple-blue.

How large a brush did you use for this?

I used Lyons-hair fresco brushes. . . . They're a specific kind of fresco brush about an inch wide—although they vary. If Diego was painting in some detail, he'd use a smaller brush, but in general he preferred to use fairly large ones, of an inch or so.

Do you remember any other sections that you did?

Well, I remember once I was very pleased because Rivera had gone off to a dinner. Frida, his wife, came [from Mexico City] to join him and to have a check-up with Dr. [Leo] Eloesser [a physician and friend] at St. Luke's Hospital. While Frida was there, people would have them both to dinner. So on this night, he had left me to paint an area, principally of barbed wire, which was in a section of illustrating Charlie Chaplin's movie *The Great Dictator*, the subject of which was Nazi persecution of Jews. Rivera left me to paint the barbed wire by myself; the next day, when Niendorff came to work, he looked at the barbed wire and said, "Boy, look at that, nobody can ever paint anything like that except Rivera." But I actually never had much of this kind of responsibility. Diego once tried me on the human figure, but I was not experienced enough to do it the way he liked, so he finished it. I did backgrounds, floors, the bay.

Did you grind the colors or did somebody else?

Emmy Lou Packard

Other assistants did that: Niendorff and a young man who was studying fresco at the California School of Fine Arts when I was. Since we needed another assistant, I got him a job on the mural. His name is Wayne Lammers. He's still around San Francisco. And so Wayne and Niendorff, or some other assistant, usually did the pouncing. I never took part in that. . . .

Did you usually go to work about the same time as Rivera?

Yes. I had a car, and I would pick Rivera up and drive him to Treasure Island. He had an apartment on Telegraph Hill—that series of white apartments that step down Telegraph Hill. After Frida arrived and was at St. Luke's Hospital, my job was to drive him out there to visit her. When she got out of the hospital, I also spent a great deal of time driving her, or both of them, around the city. It was very entertaining for me, and we had a great deal of fun. Of course, it was a marvelous opportunity for me to meet people and to see a kind of life I hadn't seen before. . . .

How long were you the painting assistant on the mural?

The fair concluded and the mural still wasn't finished, so we worked on in freezing temperatures. The building had not been heated except by the crowds that had come during the fair, and when they left, so did the heat. We had one waffle iron there, I remember, and it provided the only heat in the studio. And so the assistants hung on for, oh, a month or so after the fair closed, until the mural was finished. That was, I think, December 1940.

During the painting of the mural, various interesting things happened. For example, early one morning, Diego called me at my parents' house in Berkeley from his apartment in San Francisco. He said, "Mataron al viejo" (they killed the old man), which I knew meant that [Leon] Trotsky had been assassinated. And since he was an ardent Trotskyite at the time, Diego was afraid that there would be an attempt on his life. So the guards at the fair were tripled, and for a while everything was in a state of great excitement. He told me, by the way, about his discussions with Trotsky—it was fascinating. I wish I had had a tape recorder or had an encyclopedic memory, because nearly all the time he painted, he talked steadily to me for hours and hours and hours about his life, his artistic career, politics, millions of fascinating stories, some of them no doubt given a great deal of imaginative treatment, but I'm sure there was a great deal of fact in them too.

He told me about his quarrel with Trotsky. Trotsky believed that once socialism was achieved, this would be the end of political change. Diego told Trotsky that if Socialism or Communism were realized—if his dialectics were true—this would not be the end of change, but change would continue, and there would be some system beyond Socialism and Communism. He said that this made Trotsky furious. Diego said this was the basis of their quarrel. Now whether this was true, I don't know.

69

Krasner Lee

1908–1984

In 1942, when the painter Lee Krasner was just beginning
to make a name for herself in the art world, she knocked on
Jackson Pollock's door, not to introduce herself, but to find
out who he was. Three years later, they married.

In the mid-to-late 1960s, Dorothy Seckler interviewed
Krasner three times for the Archives of American Art. The
recordings capture the rough cadence of her Brooklyn-accented
voice and her grit. They also reveal Krasner, who admired the
art of Henri Matisse and was devoted to Pollock's vision, as a
significant link between French and American painting. Here
she talks about their first meeting, as well as radical transitions
in her life and work.

Lee Krasner, ca. 1938. Photographer unknown.
Jackson Pollock and Lee Krasner papers, ca. 1905–1984.

Lee Krasner: I was a member of the Artists' Union; we held a dance, and I met [Jackson Pollock], but a few years passed before I *really* met him.

Dorothy Seckler: So then in 1942…

Actually, I recollect meeting him, in addition to the incident [at the dance], at a show that John Graham did at the McMillan Gallery [New York City, "American and French Paintings," January 1942]. He invited three unknown Americans [to participate in the exhibition]: someone called Jackson Pollock and me, and, I believe, [Willem] de Kooning…. I ran into someone called Lou Bunce, whom I knew from the Project [WPA's Federal Art Project in New York City], and he said, "By the way, do you know this painter Pollock?" And I said, "No, I have never heard of him. What does he do, and where is he?" And he said, "Well, he's a good painter, he's going to be in a show that John Graham is doing called 'American and French Paintings.'" I said, "What is his address?" Curiously enough, at that point I was living on Ninth Street between Broadway and University, and Pollock was on Eighth Street between Broadway and University. I promptly went up to Pollock's studio and that's when I say I met Pollock for the first time…. And then, you see, after I saw Pollock and his work, I said, "I understand the third painter [in the show] is de Kooning," and he said he didn't know de Kooning, and I said, "Well, I do and I'll take you over and introduce you." So I took Pollock to de Kooning's studio. De Kooning was in a loft at that time because he was something, and that is how Pollock met de Kooning.

And you had already known de Kooning from the Project?

No, I knew de Kooning before the Project. And I knew [Arshile] Gorky years before I knew Pollock…

When you took Pollock to meet de Kooning, did they have a good rapport?

No, not necessarily. I don't think either one was impressed.

How was Pollock's work at that time?

Well, as I said earlier, a bomb exploded when I saw that first French show [earlier in this interview, Krasner talks about attending a Georges

Braque, Henri Matisse, and Pablo Picasso exhibition at the Museum of Modern Art sometime between 1929 and 1932, possibly "Painting in Paris," January 18-March 2, 1930]. The next bomb to explode was . . . when I walked into his [Pollock's] studio. There were five or six canvases around, and they had the same impact on me: something blew.

How did the show go?

Well, my own excitement around it was overwhelming. I found my work flanked by a Matisse on one side and a Braque on the other, and there was Pollock's work, which I'd seen in the studio. De Kooning's work didn't get much attention at all. Remember that in '42, American painting that was so-called "abstract" (I use the word lightly...) didn't get much attention from anybody or any place.... Nothing much came of the show in terms of outside reactions. Nothing that made a mark, in any sense.

But you obviously did get to know Pollock better —

Oh, of course.... We were married in October 1945, and moved out here [to The Springs, near East Hampton, New York] and made this our permanent residence.

And did you mutually influence each other, or did you explore certain directions together?

Our work was different. I, for one, believe art comes from art and is influenced by art; as I explained, some very positive things took place when I first saw the French paintings. Certainly, a great deal happened to me when I saw the Pollocks. Now Pollock saw my work too — I couldn't measure what effect it had on him. We didn't talk art — we didn't have that kind of a relationship at all. In fact, we talked art talk only in a shop sense.... When he did talk, it was extremely pointed and meaningful, and I understood what he meant.

Now at this point, of course, he was, I assume, working abstractly and —

Oh yes, the first paintings I saw on the occasion I described — well, some of those paintings, such as *The Magic Mirror* [1941; Menil Collection, Houston] which is up, and *Bird* [1938–41; Museum of Modern Art, New York], have been seen by many people; they've been in a lot of

Lee Krasner

exhibitions. He had long since been through with Thomas [Hart] Benton [his former teacher]. He only studied a brief time with Benton [in 1930 at the Art Students League, New York City]. As he himself said—I am quoting Pollock on this—after Benton, he went into his "black period," which I think he said lasted about three or four years, after which the first of the paintings we know today emerged…

Was he using a brush?

Well, he was, but he was using both ends of the brush so that it wasn't all that conventional, but he was not yet doing the so-called "drip."

Well, what word would you —

I don't know. I believe that's a problem for the critic or art historian to describe. . . . The word "drip"—it just drives me—it makes me very uncomfortable. Actually, [the movement of the paint] was aerial; it landed on the canvas. Now I don't know how to describe this aesthetically, but "drip" is a very bad way to explain it…. It doesn't describe anything.

In your early period out here [The Springs]—from '45 on, how did your work change in terms of content or style?

I'd worked with [Hans] Hofmann [at his New York school, from 1937 to 1940], who certainly conveyed an understanding of Cubism. I'd say my work at that point was still very much under the so-called "French influence." On meeting Pollock, I experienced another violent transition and upheaval [in my art]. And living with him and watching him work, well, certainly it had an effect, and consequently my painting changed.

How did this express itself?

… I went through a kind of black-out period, of doing paintings of nothing but built-up gray; up to that point, I had worked [only] from nature. Now let me try to explain that in a more simple way. When I took Hofmann to meet Jackson and see his work, which was before we moved here, Hofmann asked Jackson, "Do you work from nature?" There were no still lifes or models around, and Jackson's answer was,

"I am nature." Hofmann's replied, "Ah, but if you work by heart, you will repeat yourself." To which Jackson made no reply at all.

Now this is what happened to me: I had worked from so-called nature— that is, I am here and nature is out there, whether it be in the form of a woman, an apple, or anything else—but now the concept was broken and I faced a blank canvas. Well, I realized that I am nature and trying to make something happen on that canvas: this is the real transition that took place. It took me some three years; around '46 what began to emerge were very small canvases, these things around here, what I refer to as the "little images." As I gained confidence and strength, my work expanded, grew bolder.

One of the things that has struck me occasionally in talking to younger artists is how they lay claim to the heritage of Pollock, or refer to him as a father figure, even those who work in a completely different in style —

It's a good name to attach yourself to. Let's face it.... Art has always come from art. I think what Pollock's example has signified in a very valid way to many younger painters of all styles that the art is the man, or art is what you live every day although you may not put everyday objects into it. In Pollock's case, he certainly didn't. But art isn't some- thing separate from what you are. It isn't something that you go into a chapel and perform. I imagine that Pollock's art had an effect in many directions. It's hard to say.... So, to go back to myself for a moment, I still have to say that today the two painters that excite me most—or interest me most, or that still I can move from—are Matisse and Pollock. I say that with all due respect to Picasso and other painters. But these are the two sources that still are the most meaningful to me.

Lee Krasner

Robert Motherwell

1915–1991

Many of the Archives' interviews cover the broad sweep of
time, from a subject's earliest recollections to his or her current
opinions. The Archives' interview of Robert Motherwell is a case
in point. In November 1971, he spoke with Paul Cummings about
his introduction in kindergarten to abstraction. Later he talks
about studying abroad at the beginning of World War II, his
return to the United States, and his move from academia into
the art world.

Paul Cummings: When did you get interested in drawing and painting?

Robert Motherwell: When I was three, in kindergarten. You see, I'm tone-deaf; I can't carry a tune or recognize one. And a lot of kindergarten is [devoted to] dancing and singing and all of that, and I couldn't do it. So they would leave me in a corner with coloring books or with paper and paints. They had a beautiful blackboard… a real slate one, and every day at eleven o'clock the teacher would make sort of Miróesque diagrams of what the weather was that day; if it was sunny… an orange oval; if it was raining… blue lines and green grass. And I can still remember at age three suddenly grasping that forms are symbolic, that it didn't have to look like rain but that blue lines for rain were even more beautiful than an actual photograph of rain, and so on. And so I determined on the spot that somehow I would learn how to do that. Then in public school, in about the second grade, they taught me a Raggedy Ann-like schema for drawing figures in an abstract way. I also think that there must be psychologically some revulsion against realism, I mean I must have found reality realistically rendered unbearable.

Because it was — what? — too much like real life?

And I found real life horrible.

I've often wondered why there's so little early figurative work of yours.

There isn't any. I started as an abstract artist. But, you see, also at Harvard and at Stanford I studied philosophy and logic. [This]… was the height of the development of mathematical logic on the one side from Whitehead and Russell, and on the other side from Wittgenstein. And it became very clear to me… that abstract structures can be meaningful. And for most artists without such an intellectual background in those days, they were very dubious about making abstractions just for fear that they really didn't mean anything. But I knew metaphysically that by nature they meant something, so that I never had this inhibition. I mean [that for] most artists of my generation… it was a moral crisis to move from figure drawing and all the things that one had started into abstraction. But I took to it like a duck to water.

How was life at Harvard . . . as compared with, say, Stanford?

Oh, I was miserable there, really. I mean it was my first encounter with the East, with the snobbism, the anti-Semitism, the Yankee Puritanism, the hierarchies, the formalities. To me it was unendurable. Actually the year after, when I went to Paris, though I didn't know a word of French — which was one of the reasons I went — Paris seemed much more familiar to me than Cambridge and Boston did. I mean I immediately understood the people better, why they were doing what they were doing...

You went to the University of Grenoble at one point, too. Was that for summer school?

Yes. To learn French and stay in a pension. It was the year of the Munich crisis [1938]. A very dramatic summer. And then after a summer of learning schoolboy French, I went to Paris and lived for year until the war began.

You were at Oxford in England and where else?

I visited Oxford. I sailed back to America on the last [commercial] voyage of the *Queen Mary* [in 1939 it was converted into a battleship]. In Grenoble at the pension where I stayed there were four Oxford Fellows. We all knew that the war was going to start and that they would be in it. In fact all four of them were killed in the first year. It was between terms at Oxford, and they invited me to come and spend two weeks before I sailed back to America. It was a very strange, tense, melancholy, beautiful time, those two weeks with those four guys.

What kind of things happened? What was the milieu there?

Looking back at it now and knowing what happened, it was a little bit as though I had spent two weeks in a very luxurious prison with four guys who were under a death sentence. You talk and behave in an entirely different way from normal human discourse in a circumstance like that. So it was very intense, very real, and very unreal, too. I mean one of the guys wanted to be a jazz musician and thought he might be dead in a year; and was. One was a South African who wanted to be a barrister. It was — I don't know — how do you describe things like

Robert Motherwell

that? Maybe it was then that I began to get some of the tragic sense that I have that was rare in America.... In Grenoble I went out with a Czech Jewish girl. She received a notice from the Czech government just before the Munich crisis ordering her home. I remember putting her on the train and her weeping... I knew I would never see her again, that maybe she'd be dead. And I'm sure she never did survive the war.... In the late '30s, young people in Europe inevitably lived under the threat of death....

Everything was more real and closer. The bomb is a very abstract thing. Yes, sure.

Somebody pushes a button somewhere, and it happens. You went out to teach at the University of Oregon after that?

Yes. That was when I really didn't know what to do.... My friend Lance Hart from Westport was a professor at Oregon [University of Oregon, Eugene]; ... a teaching assistant, or probably an instructor,... was on leave of absence and they needed somebody. He [Hart] realized that I didn't know how to move from the academic world into the art world, which was what I really wanted. And he proposed—this would only be possible in a small friendly university like that—that they give me the job even though I wasn't ostensibly equipped. And they did. I taught courses in art. I did know the history of modern art. I gave a course in aesthetics, which I knew, philosophical aesthetics, which I knew; and so on. It was then that I really began to paint all the time.

What about the term [Abstract Expressionism], though? There are so many stories about that.

... I mean ultimately at the end of 1949 and the beginning of 1950 I invented the term "School of New York." I was asked to write the preface to the first showing on the West Coast ["Seventeen Modern Painters," Frank Perls Gallery, Beverly Hills, 1951] and in trying to find common denominators among the various people (including some people that we now would not regard as Abstract Expressionist), I realized that one couldn't aesthetically make a common denominator.... There is no such thing as Abstract Expressionism. They're a collection of individuals working with certain aspirations or whatever.

Robert Motherwell

Leo Castelli

1907–1999

In July 1969, art critic Barbara Rose interviewed legendary art dealer Leo Castelli for the Archives of American Art. In this excerpt, Castelli talks about his membership in The Club, a group of artists, poets, and critics who met to discuss the avant-garde, and their involvement in "The Ninth Street Show," a ground-breaking exhibition of new art, mostly Abstract Expressionist, that opened on May 21, 1951, in a vacant building at 60 East Ninth Street in New York City. "The Ninth Street Show" helped bring to prominence such artists as Willem de Kooning, Franz Kline, Robert Motherwell, Barnett Newman, and Jackson Pollock. Castelli paid the rent and financed the catalogue, which was designed by Kline.

Barbara Rose: I know that you were involved in setting up the Ninth Street show in 1951. Could you tell me something about that?

Leo Castelli: Well, by 1951—The Club had started in 1949 and had become a quite active affair. First of all we saw each other very often, at least once a week, and then—

What were the issues?

Well, I think that one important issue, apart from the function of the painter and all the usual stuff that is discussed among painters, was the position of the American painter versus the European painter. It was not specifically discussed, but there was a clear feeling that American painting was becoming very important. And perhaps, it occurs to me now (I never thought about it in these terms), one role I played was that I formed another kind of bridge between European and American painters; I seemed to be the only European actually, although I didn't have any official position. I was just a man about town, the only European really who seems to have understood them, and not only understood them, but really they were my great enthusiasm. For me they were just the great thing happening.

What artists particularly?

Oh, especially de Kooning, I would say, Pollock and de Kooning, these two, yes.

Already by 1951 they had emerged as —

Pollock had emerged before that for me, but de Kooning right after that. There was the Egan show [in 1948 de Kooning showed a series of black and white abstract paintings at the Charles Egan Gallery in New York] for instance, in 1949, I believe. It was the first time that people actually saw a show of de Kooning's. He never showed. He worked very little, he produced very little. And I think it was in 1949 or perhaps it was 1950. Yes, 1950 maybe, and that was a show of black and white paintings, of which the Museum of Modern Art [New York] has one, for instance. And that was really a great revelation. Soon after that, he did a painting called *Excavation* by which I was completely smitten. It is now at the Art Institute [of Chicago].

Well, what was the conception of the American artist of his role, as opposed to that of the European artist? I mean you began saying that they felt differently about their social role, let's say, or their role versus the audience.

I don't think that they had any particular notion about playing a social role. On the contrary, they rather rejected society. They considered themselves as an isolated group, as a group that was functioning within its own territory and they really didn't care very much about what people thought about them. In that sense, they were very different from the Europeans. They were involved with themselves, with the group. And they started becoming—perhaps I, Motherwell, and other people encouraged them—very proud of themselves, very sure of themselves. They felt that they were accomplishing something, that they were contributing something for the first time.

When do you think that they began to have assurance?

Oh, I would say it started right away, in 1949, at the beginning of The Club. The sense developed very rapidly right from the beginning of The Club days.

Did you find the American artists very different from the Europeans as personality types? I'm curious, since obviously you had a lot of experience with European artists.

Yes, they were very different, but that really doesn't mean very much in the sense that I had known a group that was very social and very elegant, the Surrealists. I hadn't known Picasso or Braque or any of that generation except very superficially; I didn't know how they functioned. And I suppose that our group here—de Kooning, Pollock, and so on—was more of the nature of that early group like Léger, Picasso, Modigliani. So the Americans did not surprise me as being totally different. In fact they conformed more to the image that I had of what painters should be than the Surrealists did. The Surrealists, especially Matta, whom I knew well and was a friend, were much too elegant and too involved with the social world to correspond to the real concept I had of painters and artists.

Leo Castelli

Could you tell me about why the Ninth Street Show was organized, how it came into being, and what its consequences were? How you were involved?

Well, it came into being as an outgrowth precisely of the things that you've been asking,... from the kind of feelings the American painters had in connection with their position toward the European painters. It was sort of an outburst of pride in their own strength. And we considered this show almost as the first Salon des Indépendents; this is what I called it, as a matter of fact. I was very proud of that aspect of it. I thought that never before anything of the kind had occurred in America. We had about ninety painters in it, and they were almost exclusively ... (there were a few exceptions)... involved with The Club. Not all of them members but at least people who gravitated around The Club and came often, because also non-members were admitted, of course. So the major figures there were de Kooning, who had... an important hand in the development of The Club; actually, he was much more active then in, say, group activities than he is now; he has become rather solitary, as you know. De Kooning was very important, Franz Kline was very important. [Conrad] Marca-Relli was a good organizer; he was involved in it.

Was all the painting abstract?

It was mostly... abstract, yes. People like Larry Rivers and... Grace Hartigan... became figurative right after that. Joan Mitchell stayed abstract.

Did the show make much of a splash? Was there much public reaction to it?

Well, it was a great event.... This was in an empty store, in a [building] that was up for demolition, and we paid, I think, $70 to have it for two months before it got demolished. All the painters had participated in refurbishing it, in painting this place that was almost abandoned. And it was very nice and neat. There are photographs that show you how it looked... I sort of footed most of the bill, although I didn't have much money either. I think that [in the end] I forked out as much as $200 and that seemed a tremendous amount of money, for the rent and for this catalogue that cost $25 that Franz [Kline] designed. We were all there for three days hanging and rehanging the show. All kinds of painters were dissatisfied with the way their work was hung, I remember. Rauschenberg was included, Reinhardt was included. David Smith, poor man, had a beautiful sculpture right in the window. Pollock was included, although he did not participate too much in Club activities. But he was painting.

The sense of community that obviously existed at this point —

Oh, yes, enormously.

Do you think that's missing now?

Oh, yes, completely. It doesn't exist anymore. There are groups, of course, for instance, the group that gravitates around Frank [Stella], say. And then there is the group, but much looser, that gravitates perhaps around Bob [Rauschenberg], but so many other elements that have nothing to do with painting gravitate around him that one doesn't know exactly whether he functions more as a painter or as somebody who is involved in other activities—theater, dance, etc.

Leo Castelli

Robert Rauschenberg

1925–2008

Robert Rauschenberg helped redefine American art in the 1950s
and '60s, first with his "combines"—found objects combined
with paint and arranged as sculptural collages—and then with
his silkscreened works that incorporated "ready-mades" and
found images. In 1965 Dorothy Seckler interviewed him for the
Archives. In this excerpt, he mentions his affinity with avant-
garde American composers and dancers, as well as his efforts
to make art that represented an "unbiased documentation" of
his observations. He also talks about executing his Automobile
Tire Print (1953) with the composer John Cage.

Robert Rauschenberg: I was in awe of the painters; I mean I was new in New York, and I thought the painting that was going on here was just unbelievable. I still think that Bill de Kooning is one of the greatest painters in the world. And I liked Jack Tworkov, the man and his work. And Franz Kline. But I found that a lot of artists at the Cedar Bar were difficult for me to talk to. It almost seemed as though there were so many more of them sharing some common idea than there was of me, and at that time the people who gave me encouragement in my work weren't so much the painters, even my contemporaries, but a group of musician—Morton Feldman, and John Cage, and Earl Brown—and the dancers that were around this group. I felt very natural with them. There was something about the self-assertion of Abstract Expressionism that personally always put me off, because at that time my focus was as much in the opposite direction as it could be. I was busy trying to find ways where the imagery and the material and the meanings of the painting would be not an illustration of my will but more like an unbiased documentation of my observations, and by observations I mean literally my excitement about the way in the city you have on one lot a forty story building and right next to it you have a little wooden shack. One is a parking lot and one is this maze of offices and closets and windows where everything is so crowded....

I think that I'm never sure of what the impulse is psychologically. I don't mess around with my subconscious. I mean I try to keep wide awake. And if I see in the superficial subconscious relationships that I'm familiar with, clichés of association, I change the picture. I always have a good reason for taking something out, but I never have one for putting something in. And I don't want to, because that means that the picture is being painted predigested. And I think a painting has such a limited life anyway. Very quickly a painting is turned into a facsimile of itself when one becomes so familiar with it that one recognizes it without looking at it. I think that's just a natural phenomenon....

I was very interested in many of John's [Cage] chance operations. Each one seemed quite unique to me. I liked the sense of experimentation that he was involved in. But painting is just a different medium, and I never could figure out an interesting way to use any kind of programmed activity. And even though chance deals with the unexpected and the unplanned, it still has to be organized before it can exist.... I certainly used the fact that wet paint will run, and lots of other things. It seems to me it's just a kind of friendly relationship with your materials where you want them for what they are rather than for what you could make out of them. I did a twenty-foot print, and Cage was involved in that because he was the only person I knew in New York who had a car and who would be willing to do [what I needed]. I poured paint one Sunday morning. I glued, it must have been, fifty sheets of paper together; it was the largest paper I had, and stretched it out on the street. [Cage] had an [antique] Model A Ford then, and he drove [it] through the paint and onto the paper, and he only had the direction to try to stay on the paper. And he did a beautiful job of it. Now I consider that my print. It's just like working with lithography. You may not be a qualified printer but there again, like the driver of the car, someone who does know the press very well collaborates with you and they are part of the machinery just as you are part of another necessary aspect that it takes to make anything. Would you call that accident?

◀ ◀ ◀

... [I] like seeing people using materials that one is not accustomed to seeing in art because I think that has a particular value. New materials have fresh associations of physical properties and qualities that have built into them the possibility of forcing you or helping you do something else. I think it's more difficult to constantly be experimenting with paint over a period of many, many years.

Robert Rauschenberg

Al Held

1928–2005

In 1960 painter Al Held had a breakthrough when he   93
temporarily took over Sam Francis's studio at 940 Broadway
in New York City. Responding to the new space and light,
Held changed the scale, color, and patterns of his paintings,
as well as his materials and methods. In an interview
with Paul Cummings in December 1975, Held describes this
transformation.

Al Held: Sam [Francis] got the major and best studio space. And then soon after that, Sam decided he wanted to go away... and he asked me if I would like to use his studio—this must have been 1958 or 1959—for six months. I said sure. When I moved in there, it was one of those spaces that I wasn't accustomed to, a beautiful big space, it must have been about forty or fifty by one hundred feet.... It had a regular skylight, and it was faced with frosted glass, so it had even light all over. It was an incredible studio. I had never painted in that light before. What happened was that when I moved in there I didn't know what to do.... I was sort of freaked out by this space, I was so unaccustomed to it—and I had moved all my paraphernalia over there, all my pigments and the oils and the canvas and everything else. I even did one or two paintings in the [previous] style using a palette knife. But parallel to that, I bought these big rolls of [seamless] paper...

Paul Cummings: Oh, that photographers use?

Right. Very cheap, terrible paper about ten feet high. I covered all the walls with it because I didn't want to get the place terribly dirty.... I took this acrylic, which previously I had only worked with very small on paper, and just covered the walls with it. I mean like in the space of a month I just simply took like thirty to forty feet of it and covered it with these images. They were all bright, colorful, geometric things that had this kind of overall pattern. Yes.

It was like painting a mural?

Right. I got quite excited by it. But I still was very much involved in my paintings and, as I said, did two paintings in that studio with the thick palette knife and paint and everything else. But I got much more interested in these other things. And then I thought I had made a tremendous breakthrough because it looked very fresh, very alive, very bouncy, and very jazzy. I remember talking about wanting to use "taxi-cab" colors, of getting involved in... high-key colors, which came from the paint, very involved in getting away from all that... mixed paint that I was using before and all that modulated color, and just [using]...

"taxi-cab" colors—"taxi cab" being that kind of flashy image of neon lights imagery, a whole kind of cityscape.

And straight color—I mean no mixing?

Straight color, no mixing; just straight out of the tube, out of the bottle. By the time I had completed this whole room,.... I was very excited and very, very high.... Then I stepped back. I thought I had changed my whole nature, that I had really like revolutionized myself. Then I looked at it. A lot of my old friends came in and, in absolute astonishment, sort of said: what in hell has he done? Has he given up the ghost; what is he doing with these horrible things? But I was very excited by them. They were very already loosely painted, but they were already squares and squares and squares and circles and circles and squares and triangles, a potpourri of things, lots of stuff. I remember that one day I stepped back and said to myself: I've changed everything, I've changed the color, I've changed the painting technique, I've changed the scale, I've changed everything. But then I realized that I had kept one thing and it shocked me because I hadn't realized it, which was that I had tied the painting up compositionally by still keeping overall patterns of that rhythmic kind of thing, you know, red, blue, green. So I decided if I really wanted to change, I had to break myself of that habit of tying things up that way. I began to set myself a set of axioms: "Thou shalt nots." One of the "Thou shalt nots" was never to repeat a form or a color in the same painting. And that got me...

Was this a list you wrote down or something?

... I had it in my head that, if I wanted to break that habit, I was to not do certain things. One of the primary things of what not to do was not to tie up the canvas that way. And the only way not to do it was sim-ply ... not repeat a shape or a color in the same canvas. And through that exercise, the paintings got simpler, the geometry got simpler and more evolved. And that's how the evolution started. And from that came a lot of other ideas. But it started there.

Al Held

Katharine Kuh

1904–1994

As an art dealer, educator, curator, art critic, and author,
Katharine Kuh was an early and influential advocate of
modern art. Avis Berman interviewed her in fifteen separate
sessions from March 1982 to March 1983. The transcript that
resulted, more than three hundred pages in length, is one of
the most compelling interviews in the Archives' oral history
program. There are many vignettes to choose from, as her
friends and acquaintances were numerous and her art-world
experience vast. In this excerpt, Kuh recalls her relationship
with Mark Rothko, to whom, in 1954, she gave his first museum
exhibition, at the Art Institute of Chicago, where, among other
things, she served as the museum's first curator of modern
art. The interview was funded by the Rothko Foundation.

Avis Berman: Today we're going to start talking about Mark Rothko. Why don't we start at the beginning; When you did meet Rothko?

Katharine Kuh: Well, he seemed young. Compared to his behavior in the '60s, he was really hale and hardy and hefty. And he had huge canvases that he pushed around. It was a small studio. He wasn't making any money then. He had been teaching. Let's see if he was still teaching when I first got to know him, because at one point he told me about Brooklyn College and why he wasn't teaching anymore.... All right. My first memory was what marvelous company he was that day, optimistic even though bitter about his work not being accepted. And still he believed he could do anything and I felt he could, too. I was speechless at the procession of superb paintings he pushed before me. He didn't show me any of that early stuff, the so-called Surrealist, which I want to make very clear I don't consider Surrealism at all. He showed me just a procession of high-keyed, fantastic abstractions from the early '50s. I lost my breath; he let me look as long as I wanted.

There was north light in his studio, and it was crowded and cramped because there were so many huge pictures and not enough storage space. Somehow he'd haul the stuff around and put one in front of another. I had a kind of uncomfortable chair.... Anyway, I remember sitting there absolutely bowled over, because there were so many [works] and they were so fantastic. For me it was a revelation.

Because I liked the work so much, [Rothko] naturally liked me. All artists do if you like their work. I not only liked his work, I was overwhelmed by it. He could tell. I spent the whole afternoon there and that's when we really first started to know each other.... I used to go to the Rothkos for supper when they lived in that little apartment on 53rd, was it?

Possibly. They changed the addresses a lot.

It was a tiny apartment, only about a block or two from the studio. I remember particularly when Kate [Rothko's daughter] was about a year or two old. So how long ago was that? About thirty years ago, in the early '50s, yes, that's about right. I'd go over for dinner. Mel [his wife] would have worked all day, and then she'd get home and do the cooking. We'd eat in the kitchen, which was so small that she didn't have to leave the table to stir food on the stove. All she had to do was lean over. She was a good cook.... Mark was very much in love with Mel, in love with her physically. You had that feeling all the time. She was neat, attractive, and she had a lot of spunk; she believed in herself.... When I came for dinner, he'd often haul home one of his latest paintings if I hadn't had time to go to the studio. Because I went [from Chicago] to New York intermittently on business, I used to see the Rothkos frequently. We'd have a private showing after they'd finally got Kate into bed and we'd finished supper. We'd sit in their little cramped living room and look at one of these great, blazing paintings. I still feel that his greatest contribution (Clyfford Still agreed) came from the years when he was producing the high-keyed, optimistic, glowing, almost religious paintings from about 1949–50 into the early 1960s...

Now to go back to what you were talking about earlier, colors receding and coming forward.

[Rothko] had the most marvelous ability to make warm colors recede and cool colors advance. I don't know of anyone else who really understood this kind of juxtaposition better than Mark. His paintings depended on areas of color, intensity of color, certain very self-conscious uses of texture, and of course his work was totally dependent on color. But in the end, it's the marvelous expressive quality of his color that counts. He actually invented new color arrangements, new color combinations, but it's more than color combinations—it's color intensities.

You know, he didn't like his work shown in bright light. He once told me that the ideal installation of his work was in the Phillips Collection in Washington. And he was right. It is beautiful. He didn't want his paintings in large, overpowering rooms. He wanted you to be enveloped by them, to get near them, to be totally involved in them. First, he didn't

Katharine Kuh

want them to be over-lit. He felt that the stronger the light, the more the color was dissipated, dissolved. He wanted the color to be allowed to exert enormous emotional impact. He wanted people always to have a place to sit in comfort and to have a long, quiet time to look. And that's about it. He considered his paintings as objects of contemplation.

I went to Mark's studio to select the show for the Art Institute [of Chicago], and he talked to me about how he hated having his work in big group shows, was thrilled that I wanted to have one large room of only Mark Rothko. Now I'd given one solo show before in that room, I think I told you, of Mark Tobey's work. And I told Rothko that. I said, "You're the second artist [for whom] I want to have a one-man show in my gallery at the Art Institute." He was delighted. He said, "Oh, I admire him," but he didn't say he admired his work. I don't know if he did or not. And that's a strange thing, because Tobey felt the same way about Rothko.... .

Mark felt that his work suffered immeasurably when it was seen crowded on a wall next to "ordinary" paintings. By "ordinary," he meant other people's. He wanted his work isolated because it did not work well with other people's. And he was right. In those days, most artists were not abstract, and his work was.... It was not as yet accepted, and he knew that his only hope was to have his work seen alone.

> What did he think of his show at the Museum of Modern Art, New York, the 1961 retrospective?

He wanted that show. It became an obsession with him. He had certain obsessions. One was his position in history. Two was an exhibition at the Museum of Modern Art because at that point, in the late '50s, early '60s, it was almost a necessity to have the recognition of the Museum of Modern Art. It certainly isn't anymore, but it was then. Alfred Barr [the museum's founding director] was considered the final word, and in a sense he really was. In any case, Mark felt he had to have a one-man show there.

Now this worried the life out of Mark, because MoMA took so long to recognize him.... I date many of his problems, his worst psychological problems, to that damned show.... First of all, he began to argue with the museum about whether it was to be on this floor or that floor, because [he wanted his show to be in the same location as] so-and-so....I don't know whether it was de Kooning they had given a show to before.... Jackson Pollock certainly had one before Rothko.... [Rothko] was very jealous of other artists, as you know. He demanded the exact same treatment, regardless of whether the work would look better on one floor than on another. He talked to me about the problem at great length.... But somehow or other, I think MoMA won. I don't think his show was in exactly the location he wanted.

It was a very serious show. He insisted on extremely modified light. ... They gave into him on that because they agreed with him. It was a beautiful show. Then he... changed right in front of my eyes. He stopped working altogether. Have you heard this story before?

No.

He stopped working during the show, and he hardly painted. Every day he went to that exhibition and haunted it and stood around listening to what everybody said. He became upset if they didn't understand the work or said something derogatory. He would call me and tell me about each comment. He was completely vulnerable.... I don't think that he was ever again quite the same marvelous, head-strong man.

Katharine Kuh

Tom Wesselmann

1931 – 2004

Tom Wesselmann's figurative paintings of the early 1960s
infused traditional subjects such as nudes and still lifes with
new meaning. In this excerpt from a 1984 interview with the art
historian Irving Sandler, Wesselmann talks about his first use
of collage, his approach to content, and his efforts to eliminate
the painterly and poetic from his work.

Tom Wesselmann: Two things: first, when I threw out [Willem] de Kooning, I tried to throw out every influence I was conscious of, including [Henri] Matisse. So I wanted to find a way that in a sense was the opposite of their art. De Kooning worked big; I'd work small. De Kooning—also [Jim] Dine and all the guys I knew worked sloppy; I'd work neat. It wasn't all that neat, but it was neat by comparison—

Irving Sandler: You bet it was!

They worked abstract; I'd work figurative.... At the same time, there are other things here, like I deliberately wanted to work figurative because it was the one mode that I so scorned. It was the only way to go. If you weren't going to go abstract, you were going to go figurative. But I was intrigued by the fact that I had no point of view, and I was really approaching figurative art as a naïve. I had no point of view about figurative art. I had never seen any, except that of Norman Rockwell. And— it was kind of intriguing to start off that way.

And in the same way, you introduced collage, because that's sort of anti-gestural.

I introduced collage, I think, mainly because I was impatient, *terribly* impatient, and I had no point of view about painting. That was the main thing. If you have no point of view about painting, you can't paint.... I didn't care about what I was painting. That was a very liberating thing for me, and I liked that.... I was in a position of being able to take literally anything I wanted and stick it down without caring at all.... I was literally caving in—maybe in a good way—to the influence of John Cage only just as an idea. All my collage elements in the first pieces were born with that very cavalier attitude. I had embarked on something that was so exciting to me—I mean, I could hardly contain myself—that is, I was creating my own art form. Also, I was much less inclined to care about the details. I couldn't care less about any of these things.

I remember the day quite clearly that I decided I had to throw out all this stuff. It all happened literally in one day. I went out in the morning walking in Greenwich Village, and in the gutter was this piece of gray

wood. It looked like a nice piece of wood to work on, so I took it home.
I say in one day — I guess it was more like one week, because in the
preceding days I'd run across that Pharaoh cigarette, I think, in
Washington Square and a piece of dirty yellow paper that makes [the
woman's] hair, I picked up in the gutter. [The work Wesselmann was
referring to is *Portrait Collage #1* (1959), in his studio at the time of
this interview, now in the collection of Claire Wesselmann.] A couple
of nights before, I'd gone to a Hawaiian restaurant and taken that leaf
back [on the upper right-hand corner]. I guess I can't remember whether
I did all this deliberately, or I knew what I was going to do, or I was
beginning to think I had to start doing something like this.

At any rate, in a matter of a few days I had accumulated a few collage materials. Out of envy of Jimmy Dine, who worked with staples
at the time, because he was fast. God, he was just so fast! So I wanted
to retain some of that looseness and abandon, so I imitated his use of
staples.... I still couldn't get away completely from the painterly idea.
I had to do something to the work. I put charcoal on it and smudged it
in and made it dirty here and there. Later, I construed this to be a kind
of a poetic thing I had to get rid of. I didn't want to deal in poetry....
I began to come around to the idea that was also voiced (and reinforced
in myself) by Alex Katz when I heard him say one time that he liked
his paintings to look brand new, like they'd just come out of a box.... It
was all coming together in about 1962, I guess. More and more, with
[Roy] Lichtenstein coming on the scene, and [Andy] Warhol and [James]
Rosenquist. Things were kind of clean and slick. It was just in the air
at the time.

Agnes Martin

1912 – 2004

Agnes Martin was born in Saskatchewan, Canada, and grew
up in Vancouver. She moved to the United States in 1932 and
studied art at Teachers College of Columbia University in New
York City from 1941 to 1942, and from 1951 to 1952.

Martin was living in Taos, New Mexico, when art dealer Betty
Parsons offered her an opportunity to show at her gallery in
New York City. In 1957, at Parsons's behest, Martin moved back to
the city. In this segment from an interview conducted by Suzan
Campbell in 1989, Martin talks about her return to New York in
1957, about discovering her "vision" in the form of the grid, and
why she defines herself as an Expressionist.

Agnes Martin, Ellsworth Kelly, and Robert Indiana on bikes in Lower Manhattan, 1957.
Photo by Hans Namuth. ©2008 Hans Namuth Estate. Hans Namuth photographs and papers, ca. 1952–1985.

Suzan Campbell: Why did you wait so long to begin exhibiting your work after you decided to become an artist?

Agnes Martin: For twenty years, I thought my art wasn't good enough to put out into the world.... I painted all kinds of things in those twenty years, I can tell you. But I never felt really satisfied with my work until after I went to New York and started working with the grid, which was absolutely abstract.

Tell me why you left Taos and went to New York at that time.

Betty [Parsons] bought enough paintings so that I could afford to go.

Had it been your ambition to return to New York?

She wouldn't show my paintings *unless* I moved to New York.

So Betty enticed you away from Taos with the promise of a show and the purchase of work?

Yes. And more shows.

When you got to New York, where did you locate yourself?

I lived on Coenties Slip. It's below Wall Street, and I had a view of the [East] river, and I paid $45 a month.

Were you in a loft?

In a loft, yes.

Were there other artists working there?

Yes. Ellsworth Kelly and I were in the same building. He had the top floor with the skylights. Then, just down the street were [Robert] Indiana and Jack Youngerman; and around the corner on Pearl Street were [Robert] Rauschenberg, Jasper Johns, and Larry Poons. And then later came James Rosenquist. I think that's all.

◀ ◀ ◀

Agnes, tell me about the grid. The grid seems to have coincided with your arrival in New York.

No, not quite. I had one show, my first [at the Betty Parsons Gallery in 1958]. I was not using the grid. No, it took me two years. In 1960—I guess it was just one year—I made my first grid on a canvas that was six by six feet, and so I continued to work with that measurement. I've been painting six by six feet [canvases] now for thirty years.

> To the casual or uninitiated viewer of your work, it appears that it was a big jump, both philosophically and aesthetically.

Yes. It's a big jump into completely abstract work like mine, which is not abstracted from nature, but really abstract. Abstraction describes subtle emotions that are beyond words, like music, which, you know, represents our abstract emotions. All music is completely abstract, and so it's a big leap to go from objective work into abstract work.... When I first made a grid, I happened to be thinking of the innocence of trees [laughs], and then this grid came into my mind and I thought it represented innocence (I still do), and so I painted it and then I was satisfied. I thought, this is my vision.... .

[My paintings are] beyond words. That's what makes them abstract. But my [current] dealer [Arnold Glimcher] encourages me to name the paintings. He claims that it helps the observer respond to them. So sometimes I name them.

> Does it bother you if an observer, or viewer, of your paintings doesn't see in them what you felt when you were making them?

No, it doesn't bother me at all. I just want people to have their own response to the paintings.

◀ ◀ ◀

> Agnes, I know you didn't hang out with people the way that many of us socialize, but which artists in New York did you consider yourself close to in a friendship kind of way?

Well, I guess I was closest to Ellsworth Kelly. I was pretty good friends with Indiana; I was friends with all of them.

> Did you feel that being in that milieu, with all those artists working quite hard, helped you as an artist? Did it reinforce your determination or goals?

No. No. As a matter of fact when you say we didn't hang out, we were very good friends when we met, you know, but when you finish a

Agnes Martin

painting you have to do something else, to get it off your mind. We all did the same thing, like we crossed [the East River] on the ferry and went to Prospect Park—things like that—but we went alone, we didn't go together.

Is that right?

Yes, because it's better not to get involved and argue and talk if you're really seriously moving ahead. But I was interested that they did the same things I did.

You mean the way they lived their lives?

Walked across the Brooklyn Bridge.

Is that right?

Yes, we all did the same things but we did them alone.

You didn't know. These were spontaneous occurrences happening at the same time?

No, it's just the best thing to do when you stop painting. The best thing in the world to do is cross the Brooklyn Bridge.

◀ ◀ ◀

Do you consider yourself an Abstract Expressionist?

Yes, I do.

I'm glad to hear that. I read that you don't. I was surprised that in New York you were perceived for a while as a Minimalist.

Yes.

I know you were in a show with nine other artists at the Virginia Dwan Gallery in New York.

Yes. They were all Minimalists, and they asked me to show with them. But that was before the word was invented. And I liked all their work, so I showed with them. And then, when people started calling them Minimalists, they called me a Minimalist, too.

And what did you think about that?

Well, I let it go, but—I didn't protest, but I consider myself an Abstract Expressionist.

I'm not sure that Minimalism as an art movement ever actually realized

Oh, yes. The truth is that what they were was non-subjectivists. They wanted not to make any personal decisions in their work. And they were idealists, like the Greeks. The goal was perfection such as we have in our minds. The Greeks knew that we cannot make a perfect circle but in our minds we can see a perfect circle, and so they said that perfection is in the mind. But the Minimalists wanted to be impersonal, and they thought the more impersonal, the more effective, which is logical [laughs].

Do you feel that this describes your work?

No.

What's the difference between you and those who came to be called Minimalists?

Well, my work is more expressive, I don't know exactly what the expression is, but it just has more human expression. That's why I say that I'm an Expressionist. Before I start, I have a vision in my mind about what I'm going to paint, and that's what the vision is, and that's what I paint.... When I make a mistake, I make a mistake in scale. Then it's no good at all unless I get it exactly to scale. See, I have a little picture in my mind, and I have to make it into a six-foot canvas. So I often make mistakes in scale.... The object of painting is to represent concretely our most subtle emotions. That's my own definition.

Agnes Martin

Sheila Hicks

Born 1934

Current thinking about the globalization of contemporary art has finally caught up with the formidable fiber artist Sheila Hicks. Inspired by the textiles of many cultures, Hicks developed her own international vocabulary in fiber. Her complex works range from potholder-sized weavings to sculpture, tapestries, site-specific public art commissions, and environmental art of reclaimed clothing. She studied painting with Josef Albers at Yale University, traveled on student grants to South America and France, and lived in Mexico from 1960 to 1965 before moving to Paris, where she has maintained a studio for more than forty years.

In 2004 Monique Lévi-Strauss, writer and wife of anthropologist Claude Lévi-Strauss, interviewed Hicks at her home in Paris for the Archives of American Art. In this excerpt, Hicks talks about her early experiments with weaving and trying to find her niche in the art world.

Monique Lévi-Strauss: Sheila, now we're back in March 1960, and you've landed in Mexico because you are about to have a baby. Would you please go on from there?

Sheila Hicks: I turned my thoughts to living in one peaceful place with one person, having a child, and making my home environment something wonderful. I had been out in space a good long while, and I was weary and wanted to settle down. Weaving and textiles became more and more important to me. I painted intermittently, and I drew, but mostly I looked for and found people working with textiles. [The German-Mexican painter] Mathias Goeritz invited me to teach, so I kept my hand in creative communication, something I thought I was going to avoid. Two Thursdays a month I taught design and color to architecture students at the Universidad Autónoma in Mexico City. It took me to the city, which was three and a half hours from where I lived. I saw exhibitions and met people and had exchanges. Otherwise, I was with the indigenous population in the valley of Taxco el Viejo.

I began making textiles for my own amusement, and for others, too—weaving large-scale. I worked with [the American weaver] Polly Rodriguez, who had a workshop in Taxco and with [the Mexican weaver] Rufino Reyes, from Mitla, near Oaxaca, who would come up and sell his wares. Together we created new designs.... I became rather well acquainted with [the Mexican architect] Luis Barragán. He encouraged me to keep working on textiles and gave me ideas for things he wanted me to weave for a convent he was designing and for his own house.

These were large-scale projects?

They seemed large to me—larger than miniatures, things that could be made on a domestic scale. I was already making everything for my own house—bedcovers, cushions, upholstery, carpets.

Did you have a loom in Taxco?

I improvised by turning tables upside down and making them into four-post looms, attaching bars to the legs of the tables. At about that time, my husband started becoming annoyed at how much time I was spending on this; he thought I should be taking care of the garden and other aspects of country living. He challenged me: "Enough with these potholders. Why don't you show them to somebody and get an evaluation to see if they're worth anything, because it's absorbing a lot of your energy and time and maybe you should get back to painting."

So he didn't believe so much in your weaving, less than Luis Barragán.

Less than Mathias Goeritz, less than Luis Barragán. Nobody believes in weaving if you think the weaver knows how to paint. Why are they losing time weaving?

Well, somebody who owned a gallery and who could exhibit your weavings and sell them would believe in it.

Do you think such a gallery existed?

I'm asking.

Truthfully, I thought along those lines myself. I took my weavings—it wasn't very hard to carry them, easier than paintings—and showed them to Antonio Souza, who had a gallery in Mexico City [Galería Antonio Souza]. He said, "Yes, let's make an exhibition." That was my first exhibition of this kind of work ["Tejidos," 1961].

I also took them up to New York. Mathias Goeritz had given me the name of Greta Daniel at the Museum of Modern Art. She was a curator in the department of architecture and design. She was from Bottrop, the same town in Germany where [my teacher Josef] Albers had come from. I get into moods sometimes—a sort of fury. I flew to New York [in 1961] and called the Museum of Modern Art, saying that I was at the airport and that I urgently needed to meet Greta Daniel. She said, "Well, then, come right over."

I spread out my work. Remember these were just small pieces, about 25 by 15 centimeters [10 by 6 inches]. Some were slightly larger, maybe 35 by 30 centimeters [14 by 12 inches]. I had a series of them, layers, like pancakes or crepes.

Most of these weavings must have been with four selvages.
Am I correct?

Yes. They were made on a small loom that I had improvised; I'd taken painting stretchers and pounded nails in the two ends and then stretched yarns between the nails. I was using techniques that I had observed in Pre-Incaic textiles, and I was trying out things and learning as I went along. The colors were not Peruvian, nor like tapestries.

At that time, what fiber did you use?

Cotton and wool.

Of course, if you made the work in Mexico, you were using dyed fiber.

Yes. But often I used undyed handspun wool that was very crusty and tough-looking. If it was dyed, it was either with natural dyes or aniline dyes, in brilliant, shocking colors.

So those were Mexican colors?

No, they were *my* colors: a mix of Mexico, Albers, and France.... They were sometimes very subtle; I loved the paintings of [Édouard] Vuillard and [Pierre] Bonnard, so at times I would use mellow tones, not always high contrast or shocking ones....

I'm sure Mathias had written [Greta Daniel] a letter, because she was so nice, and she introduced me to Arthur Drexler, who was the head of the architecture department and to Alfred Barr, the director of the museum [in 1961, Barr was actually the former director, but was still affiliated with the museum]. They must have received a letter announcing the arrival from Mexico of some exotic girl with her potholders or something. They could have been making fun of me and just wanted to see whom Mathias was sending to them. They gave me a ticket to go and have lunch in the cafeteria on the upper floor of the museum. When I returned, they had talked and decided to buy something.... Rather than the colors, they seemed more interested in the structures of the monochrome weavings, the textures, and the way I was moving the yarn to sort of write individual lines. I was handpicking each row of the weaving. The pieces were of predetermined sizes. All the edges were finished.

They were almost identical, front and back. Texture would spring loose, then reintegrate, almost like drawing with yarn.

Alfred Barr said, "Can you make this larger?" Of course. I set about trying to make larger ones. I counted how long it would take me. Now I felt validated in the work that I liked doing. Don't forget, I had a baby [daughter, Itaka Marama Schlubach] and being with her and sitting and weaving were compatible. I had many hours to myself. Also I mobilized a few people who worked on the ranch to help me in their spare time. I think that's why my husband became annoyed; they should have been out clearing weeds, pruning the lemon trees, and getting his supper ready.

About how many people were weaving?

The number grew maybe from three to six or seven.... I wanted my weavings exhibited in a New York gallery. Well, that was a wake-up experience. I showed them to Bertha Schaefer. She bought one made of short lengths of irregularly spun knotted wool [*Rufino*, 1961], but that was it. "Thank you, it's charming." I showed them to John Lefevre at his gallery, where he was exhibiting the work of the Swiss painter Julius Bissier. I liked Bissier. Lefevre said, "Let me borrow these, and come over to my house to a cocktail party tonight. I want to show them." I went, but it was a cocktail party with three men only vaguely interested in my weavings....

I didn't realize what I was facing. The art public was not going to respond to this work: it was the craft public that would. I showed my weavings to the American Craft Museum in New York [then the Museum of Contemporary Crafts, now the Museum of Arts and Design]. Each time I'd visit someone, they'd give me the name of someone else. Go and see [writer and editor] Cora Carlyle at *American Fabrics* magazine. See Jack Lenor Larson [textile designer]. Make friends with Mildred Constantine, [a curator] at the Museum of Modern Art, who loves Mexico, [and] Wilder Green, an architect. I would get a positive response, but it didn't go much further than that, just "Be sure and show me your new work when you come back."

Back in Mexico, I received a letter in 1963 asking if I would like to exhibit in a group show at the American Crafts with four other artists. They were preparing a show called "Woven Forms." That would have been my first museum presentation. I thought, that's a downer, so I said "Thank you, but no thank you. I don't want to be in the crafts museum in a group show." I found out that the museum staff had gone to the Museum of Modern Art, which was just next door, and borrowed my work that was in their collection to include in the show. So it was in my interest to cooperate and give them biographical information, photos, and to just swallow hard. I didn't see the exhibition until the last week.

There I discovered other fiber work that I liked very much—work by Claire Zeisler and Lenore Tawney—so much so that on my way back to Mexico I stopped in Chicago to see my family, and I looked up Claire Zeisler, who lived there. We became close friends, working, traveling, and exhibiting together, thanks to that show.

That was in 1963? And did that show travel, or was it another show that did?

Part of the show traveled. I had been in contact with the Kunstgewerbe Museum in Zurich; its director, Erika Billeter, decided to do a show and invite—at first, I thought she was inviting just me. How self-centered artists are! She was inviting me, *plus* Claire Zeisler and Lenore Tawney, but not the other two artists included in the New York show [Dorian Zachai and Alice Adams]. From then on, I was grouped with Lenore and Claire. They were much older, but their work was youthful in attitude. It ended up that we three never got out of lockstep for the next twenty years. It just kept perpetuating: the three of us would be invited to participate in textile-art shows. Lenore exhibited in New York at the Willard Gallery. I have letters from her describing how she was struggling to show her art. Claire had different kinds of options. She never struggled, except in later life when she was intent on confirming her identity as an artist.

Did you go to Europe when your work was shown in Zurich?

Yes, I started to migrate to Europe and slowly to leave Mexico....

And you took your daughter to Zurich?

I took my daughter everywhere. She was too young to protest. [Laughs.] She saw a lot of places; we were inseparable, and she was charming and made friends on trains or planes. It became clear to me that the rest of my life was not going to be spent on the ranch in Mexico; I decided to leave and come to France.... I couldn't envision what my niche would be if I lived in the United States. I was not trying to live like an artist. I think I just wanted to do my art. I had to find a way to finance this exodus from Mexico and land in France. I went to Knoll Associates, the furniture design company. I showed them my work, my experiments for upholstery, curtains—they were called casements—even carpets and panels. Florence Knoll [designer and founder of the firm] came to the meeting. Their interest in me had nothing to do with how I looked [Hicks was beautiful], because Knoll was a beautiful woman; nor did it have anything to do with people writing letters of introduction on my behalf.

Knoll gave an order to a man sitting at the table. I later learned he was the president of the company [Cornell Deckert], but of course she had formed the company. She said, "I don't want her to leave this office without your giving her a contract to work with us." And he said, "But she lives in Mexico." She answered, "It doesn't matter where she lives; she will send us ideas and designs and show us her work regularly." So I landed a consulting contract with Knoll for a modest monthly fee, but it was still three times more than my student grant after graduate school to France. That was the first, solid financial backing I could count on, and with that I could move from Mexico to France.

119

Sheila Hicks

Jay DeFeo

1929 – 1989

The legendary curator Walter Hopps wrote that Jay DeFeo's   121
masterpiece, The Rose *(Whitney Museum of American Art,
New York), is "one of the most powerful images conveyed by
a creative artist in our time." The sheer monumentality of the
painting, as well as DeFeo's devotion to it, inspires wonderment.*

Based in San Francisco, DeFeo began The Rose *in 1958
and worked on it in earnest for eight years. The eleven-by-
seven-and-a-half-foot composition with its highest surface
thickness measuring eight inches, weighs 2,300 pounds.
In its long, meandering evolution,* The Rose *has become an
icon of San Francisco's Beat culture.*

*In this excerpt from an interview conducted by Paul
Karlstrom in 1976, DeFeo talks about the evolution of* The Rose
*and how Hopps had it moved from her studio on Fillmore
Street to the Pasadena Art Museum in November 1965. However,
it was not exhibited there until 1969.*

Paul Karlstrom: Maybe we really should talk about *The Rose* and something about *The Rose* and its conception — of the painting and the ideas.

Jay DeFeo: As I said before, I just draw a complete blank when somebody asks me about all the philosophical and metaphysical things that it might imply as an idea. I'll let *The Rose* speak for itself in that regard. But as far as its conception is concerned, see all of my early work is a kind of a building up of a vocabulary that kind of went into the conception of the thing, the one thing. And not too long before starting the painting, I was doing what I considered in my imagination a series of paintings based on — we were all interested in reading about mountain climbing and things of that nature — but I think the subject matter just kind of lent itself to the Abstract Expressionist movement.

Mountain forms and jagged peaks?

Yes, that sort of thing. James Kelly was doing the same. Wally [Hedrick, the artist's husband] was interested in reading about those things. At any rate that kind of imagery was the beginning of my very heavy black and white period, let's say. I think some of that influenced *The Rose* a bit. But at the beginning, actually the original canvas was painted over one of those old mountain paintings, one of the ones that just never quite made it.

Did you start out then with the idea that a new painting was going to grow out of this image?

No, no. It was just an old canvas that was handy. As a matter of fact, there was another one-night-stand painting underneath [the mountain image] called *Jacob and the Angel*, which never came off either [laughs]. That was painted out. And then I got the notion of an idea that had a center to it. And to digress just a trifle again, too, Paul, I had been working on some very large drawings of roses. Huge ones. Eleven-foot ones, a couple of which were in the Dilexi show ["Jay DeFeo," Dilexi Gallery, San Francisco, July 6 – August 31, 1959]. And the rest of them were finally destroyed. But when I started *The Rose*, I had no notion of "the rose" about it. The title came later. It was just a

painting. And all I knew ... was that it was going to have a center. When
the canvas started, it wasn't symmetrical. I had been working on it for
six months when Dorothy Miller [a curator at the Museum of Modern
Art, New York] saw it; she reproduced it at this stage in the catalogue
for her show at MoMA, "Sixteen Americans" [1959]. After six months of
working on the thing, I decided that the canvas should be symmetrical
and that it wasn't really quite the right proportions. So with the help
of Bruce Conner and Wally and a couple of other good buddies, I trans-
ferred the original canvas and glued it onto a larger format, which
it's on presently. So the work started expanding beyond the original
canvas. That's when work *really* started in earnest.

The Rose is almost like a lifespan, a kind of chronology of different
stages. The first stage, for instance—that reproduced in the [MoMA]
catalogue—it's almost like an infancy period, and one could consider
it almost complete in itself. If I had had—I don't know whether I
would have done it that way—somehow or another, all this had to go
on a single canvas—but if I had had the facilities and a large number
of canvases, I could have easily had a complete showing of the different stages of the metamorphoses it went through, as it were. Anyway,
I'd say there was that beginning stage. And then it got into a very, very
geometric stage—a crystalline sort of thing. In this period, it was reproduced in *Holiday*, as well as in *Look* magazine. At this point, there
were no curved forms whatsoever. It was very, very geometric. There
were even sticks introduced to support it in a very geometric way. But
then that didn't seem satisfactory to me, although that did seem a
complete stage in itself. It held up visually as another version, let's say,
of the concept. Then it started getting much more organic in character,
which pleased me. Although the structure of the thing remained, the
interweaving of organic shapes began.... It actually went *far* beyond
the finished state that you know it as now. It went even into ... a super
kind of baroque period.... Very, very *flam-boy-ant*. I really wasn't
aware of how flam-boy-ant it had become. I had been so involved in

123

Jay DeFeo

the thing, and all of a sudden I walked into my studio one day, and the whole thing seemed to have gotten completely out of hand. I felt that it really needed to be pulled back to something more classic in character. That again, the kind of paring back of the thing. Every time this happened, it was the work of a sculptor as well as the work of a painter, because of the nature of the material. It actually had to be carved and hacked. It was a very hard physical job, as well as a very difficult job.

How did you carve it?

Well I just had to hack away at it, Paul. It was done with a combination of building up and paring back at every stage of the game. More than once, I worked the surface back down to the original canvas. Some... think that it was just gradually built up over the years, and so it was, but more than once, it was scraped down to the canvas. And the whole thing had to be commenced from scratch.

Was there any chance or hope at the time that the Pasadena Art Museum would purchase the work?

Well, yes. I think Walter [Hopps] very much wanted it for the Pasadena Museum. Now we're getting into the complications that ensued.... Walter was so completely dedicated to the goal of having *The Rose* at the Pasadena Museum that no expense and no sacrifice was too great to achieve this. I only found out only later that the project was costing the museum far more than it could actually afford. I... was caught between the devil and the deep blue sea, as it were. It's necessary here to say of course that, as soon as the painting was removed [from my studio], this triggered off the breakup of my marriage, and Wally moved over to Ross [a small town north of San Francisco], where all of our belongings were, but I had nowhere to go and so the idea at the time was that I would go with the painting to Pasadena and stay down there for a brief period and attempt to put on the final details, to do the final finishing, if that were possible. So when Walter came up and conferred with Wally about moving the thing—this is before Wally and I knew that we were breaking up, however [laughs]—so the first movers they contacted was Bekins. Just to give Bekins a plug here, they did a magnificent job.... They had never handled anything like this before; *The Rose* had to be wedged out of that very, very tight front window with no leeway whatsoever. This was the marvelous drama of the thing. I think that Walter was somewhat responsible for this. A *small* truck could have done the job, but Bekins sent over the biggest van that it had to offer [laughs]. And the whole thing went down to Pasadena. And getting back to the poor Pasadena Museum again and the expenses. Nowadays that doesn't seem like a hell of a lot—compared to what *The Rose* has cost everybody, but $2,000 for moving the painting from San Francisco to Pasadena was a hell of a lot of money.... I wonder what it would cost now to move it down to Pasadena. But anyhow, this was the first thorn in the side of the Pasadena Museum when they got the bill for moving the painting. And not only that, it got me too [laughs].

Jay DeFeo

Robert C. Scull

1917–1986

The New York City taxi-fleet owner Robert C. Scull began
collecting art in the 1950s, concentrating on the Abstract
Expressionists. By the end of that decade, he became interested
in the work of younger artists, such as Jasper Johns, Robert
Rauschenberg, James Rosenquist, and Andy Warhol. In the
1960s, he assembled a world-famous collection of Pop and
Minimal art, quickly becoming as well a celebrated participant
in the New York art scene.

In 1972, one year before Scull sold at auction fifty works
from his collection for $2.2 million, Paul Cummings interviewed
him at length about his relationships with artists and dealers
and the development of his collection. The interview captures
the force of Scull's personality, as well as his passion for Pop Art
and his early support of Earthworks.

Robert C. Scull in the Metropolitan Museum of Art, New York City, ca. 1974.
Photograph by Cosmos. Robert Scull papers, 1968–1983.

Robert C. Scull: Oh, yes. I became immediately involved with [Sidney]
Janis and [Leo] Castelli [both located in New York City]. I started to
buy out nearly all the shows: the [Mark] Rothko show, the [Franz] Kline
show, all the Abstract Expressionists from Castelli. I found my man
there: Jasper Johns. He and I must have had some rendezvous set up for
us [by fate], because nobody bought from his first show but me ["Jasper
Johns," Leo Castelli Gallery, January 1958]. In 1958 he was looked upon
as some sort of screwball who was trying to make it without joining the
Tenth Street group [first-generation Abstract Expressionists and other
up-and-coming artists who, in the 1950s, showed at new galleries on
Tenth Street in the East Village]. I bought out nearly the whole show,
even though Castelli must have thought it was a pretty vulgar thing to
do. I supported Johns after that by buying nearly everything of his I
could. And Rauschenberg. I knew that a tremendous thing was happening with these two artists. They were opening up the whole...world.
After Johns and Rauschenberg, anything was possible.... Like
Duchamp, Johns has taken objects out of their context, and with his
Beer Can, his *Flag*, and his *Target*, he's given us an experience so
tremendous that, if he never painted another picture, he has already at-
tained immortality because of the way his mind works. Look what he's
done. In the middle of Abstract Expressionism, look at what the man
has done!

◀ ◀ ◀

Did you find some of the things you acquired difficult to live with, or to
have around, or to think about?

No. No. I loved all of it. I loved it. As a matter of fact, as soon as I found
Pop Art, [examples] came right into my home. I lived on Long Island
then, in a beautiful home on the water. And along with my Abstract
Expressionist works, there were now the Oldenburgs and.... They
moved right in, and they were just a pleasure to have around. As a

matter of fact, I was so involved with Pop that it eclipsed my awareness of Abstract Expressionism for a year or two. But I always had around the very best of Barney Newman, the finest paintings of Kline and de Kooning. So I always respected them. But I was very, very excited about the new artists.

But you've not continued collecting de Kooning, for example, have you?

No. When de Kooning became part of history, I didn't want to go back to—I don't fill stamp albums with my paintings. That doesn't interest me. I'm only involved with my own total experience, with what's on the canvas. I love de Kooning, but I can't see myself now paying $150,000 for a de Kooning because there are other things that I can love.... And also I've become aware of the younger artists. In other words, it's a special trip for me to be involved with them. And also it's part of my enjoyment of where I am in art.

So you never go back really?

No. I like the new things that are happening.

There wasn't really much publicity about you when you were collecting Abstract Expressionists, was there? Didn't that really start with Pop?

It got off the ground with Pop. Pop was not an isolated art. It came with an entire scene in which everything was Pop. It was truly an expression of its moment: the clothes, people, vinyl, movies, fads. . . . As a matter of fact, it was so new that it took our breath away. The high luster of it was the way we were living: the parties we were giving, the good times, the scene, the breaking of old mores and traditions. Living was swinging. There were no more restrictions. Everything was possible. And that's what we learned from Pop.

You really commissioned many works of art. When did you start that?

Right from the beginning. I think one of the first was a painting by Franz [Kline]. And I asked John Chamberlain to do a sculpture. I commissioned three paintings by Johns: *Number Five*, *Target*, and *Double Flag*. It became such a normal thing for me to do when I became friend-

Robert C. Scull

ly with an artist. Jasper was working on the number paintings. I said to him, "Jasper, would you paint a nice six-foot '5' for me?" He laughed and said, "What do you mean, paint a '5'? What for?" I said, "Well, you're painting numbers. '5' is my favorite number." He looked at me like I was crazy and said, "You know, I don't do that. I don't paint numbers." And then a couple of weeks later, he said, "You know, that's not a bad idea." It was thrilling to see a painting develop that way.

How did the Double Flag project come about?

I knew that Jasper had painted a flag. I wanted one. He said he couldn't make the same painting [twice], but he might consider a double flag, which he had had on his mind for quite some time. I said, "Well, will you do one for me?" He said, "Okay." That's how it came to be. In other words, he had been thinking about that painting, but he had never really gotten into it. And, you know, Jap [Jasper] was not a man who took on commissions very easily. But we were very friendly, Jap and I. And he also was very happy that I had supported his work so early on. He was cognizant of the fact that I had been crucial to his career at that time. I bought drawings; I bought everything I could find.

◀ ◀ ◀

You've mentioned the Warhol portrait. How did that happen? That's the one with the thirty-two —

Thirty-six. *Ethel Scull Thirty-Six Times* [1963; Whitney Museum of American Art, New York]. I was very friendly with Andy at the time, going around with him a great deal. I had already bought a number of his pictures. I said to Andy that I'd like to give my wife a birthday present. "How about a portrait of her?" He said, "That's a great idea. I'll think about it." A couple of weeks later, he called up my wife and said he wanted her to be photographed. I thought he was going to take her to a very fancy photographer. I learned later that he took her down to 42nd Street and made hundreds of pictures, these little —

Quarter machines.

Yes. Automatic pictures. That was in early April. Throughout the summer, all my friends kept telling me that they'd visited Andy's studio and they were walking all over my wife. I said, "What are you talking about?" They said, "Well, he's making pictures, all sizes, and he said he wasn't happy with them...." In October I said, "Andy, my wife's birthday is coming soon." He said, "I know. I know. I know. I'll have it in time." A couple of days before her birthday, he called me and asked, "Will you be home?" I said, "Why?" I had almost given up hope of ever seeing the painting. He said, "It's finished." I was very, very pleased with it. I think it's one of his most successful portraits. His *Jackie Kennedy* repeats the same image, and it is rather somber. Most of his other portraits do not attain the psychological excitement of the colors [one finds in *Ethel Scull Thirty-Six Times*]. . . . It's really a wonderful, wonderful portrait.

How did your wife like it?

Loved it. Loved it.

◀ ◀ ◀

When you started all of this, did you have any idea that these paintings were going to become as sought after and expensive as they did?

Your question requires an answer with a degree of honesty; otherwise, we're wasting time. When I bought... the Abstract Expressionist works, I thought that, with a certain degree of luck, they'd be worth twice as much. Maybe a Kline that I paid $800 for would one day be worth $1,200 or $1,500. And that's where I was at. What they were going to be worth really didn't weigh very heavily on me. The freedom with which I bought—you must understand that I couldn't have bought the things I did if I had been doing it for appreciation of value. What fool would have bought what I did?

In those days, yes.

So you have to understand that this was no consideration whatsoever. When I bought a Kline, I said to myself, "God, if ever I need any money, I hope that at least I'll get my money out of it." But I never thought that it would go up in value ten or twenty times. I was just as dumbfounded as the rest of the world. As a matter of fact, prices have gone to such

Robert C. Scull

ridiculous lengths I can't begin to tell you. A Johns today is spoken of in terms of $150,000. It's so wild, I can't believe it. It's just absolutely ridiculous. What shall I say—that I'm terribly unhappy about it? No, I'm flabbergasted at what's happened. I had no idea. Of course if I had had an idea that this was the name of the game, I wouldn't have bought these things. I would have bought safer things.

◀ ◀ ◀

I'm curious also about some of the recent things, like Michael Heizer's things [Nine Nevada Depressions, 1968]. I mean, you can't roll up the desert and put it in a box or do anything with it.

In April 1968, Heizer wrote me a letter in which he said, "My name is Michael Heizer. I'm a sculptor. I make sculpture in the desert. I carve in the desert certain patterns" . . . and "I want you to finance them." At first I thought he was absolutely crazy. I went down to see him. He had a huge map of Nevada. He showed me that he wanted to make nine pieces of sculpture starting from the top [of the state and going] all the way down to Las Vegas, [a stretch of] 540 miles, and he said he wanted to carve these in the desert. I said, "Why? Who will see them?" He looked at me and said, "Well, they'll be there. If you ever want to go to see them, they'll be there." I said, "It will take some effort to see them." He said, "You'll need a helicopter... because a small plane can't land there." I listened to him and I suddenly realized that he was talking about the purest kind of art there is, an art that I could own but could not sell, that would even be a hardship for me to see, but nevertheless own-ing it would give me some kinship with it, even if weren't on a wall in my house. I said, "Go ahead and do it. I'll pay for it." I thought it would come to a couple of thousand dollars.... In August he called me and said, "Well, I'm all set." I said, "Set for what?" Then the bills started to come in like you'd never believe.... I said, "What the hell is that man doing out there?" So I fly out. He meets me in Vegas... and he takes me to my sculpture in the desert. We landed on one of those dry lakes thirty miles outside of Vegas (there's nothing but miles and miles of desert).

When I saw this piece of sculpture in the ground, ... I began to realize that this was some of the most important sculpture in the world; and that it wasn't necessary that I be able to take it home to Fifth Avenue.... I realized that Heizer's a genius....

Robert C. Scull

Chuck Close

Born 1940

The Archives of American Art's interview with Chuck Close
reveals him to be an articulate, thoughtful, sensitive, and
engaging artist who, for one thing, regrets that his nickname,
Chuck, stuck— he would have preferred to be called "Charles."
    As a youth, Close struggled with dyslexia, but later
flourished as an art student. He studied at the University of
Washington and then from 1962 to 1964 attended graduate
school at Yale University, where he specialized in printmaking.
He and a remarkable number of his classmates at Yale—Janet
Fish, Nancy Graves, Brice Marden, and Richard Serra—all
rose to prominence in the late 1960s. Using a variety of media
and techniques, Close reinvigorated portraiture with his
monumental faces based on photographs. In this excerpt from
an interview conducted by Judd Tully in 1987, Close talks about
his time at Yale and the labor-intensive process of making his
fingerprint portraits.

Chuck Close: [When I was a child,] everybody looked through the Sears, Roebuck catalogue. The first thing that I can ever remember asking for out of the catalogue was a professional oil-paint set. I can still smell those paints. In fact I opened a tube of paint recently that had the same smell that that Sears Roebuck paint had. I guess it was cheap oil. God! A waft hit me; it was the smell of my childhood. But I had also very elaborate puppet-show things; we made our own puppets, staging, and backgrounds. My father helped me. And I had a thing for model railroads—first a Lionel and then HO [a 3.5 mm to one-foot scale]—for which I made all the mountains. My mother sewed costumes. I did a lot of theater stuff. For my magic act, my parents got me a top hat and tails at the Salvation Army. So they were very supportive of anything that I wanted to do.

Judd Tully: So when did you decide to be an artist?

Always wanted to be an artist since I was four. Always. Now in high school, I got interested in sports cars and stuff like that, so I thought I'd better be a commercial artist (practicality reared its ugly head). So I entered college to become a commercial artist, but you have the same foundation courses for painting as for commercial art.

◀ ◀ ◀

[My conservatism] carried right through graduate school. We [Close and his fellow graduate students at Yale] were very suspicious of everyone. When [Robert] Rauschenberg came up to do a group crit, my roommate—Bill Hokkis—and I went and bought a live chicken, because Rauschenberg had done a combine with a stuffed chicken [*Odalisk*, 1955–58; Museum Ludwig, Cologne]. We took the chicken to class and put it underneath a box on top of a pedestal and tied its foot to the box. Rauschenberg arrived, and then Hokkis lifted off the box, and everybody laughed. Rauschenberg laughed. The chicken, which had been asleep in the box, stood up, looked around, and just as Rauschenberg started to give a standard art crit, the chicken produced an unbelievable streak of shit, which spurted across the room as if to comment on what Rauschenberg was saying. [Laughs.] It was incredibly funny, but we were very suspicious of people like Rauschenberg.

At that time, was he red hot?

Yes. 1962. 1963, maybe. Frank Stella came up in 1963, I believe. Imagine this: During Frank Stella's lecture, Richard Serra got up, outraged by him. Called him a fake, a fraud. Stormed out of the lecture. So you can see that we were very conservative. We were not, as an art school, on the cutting edge. We were not the equivalent of what was going on in New York at the time. The faculty invited Rauschenberg and Stella. When we were asked whom we wanted, we said Edwin Dickinson.

◂ ◂ ◂

I remember when [Philip] Guston came [to Yale as a visiting artist]. I had made a painting that, at the time, I liked quite a bit. I was just finishing it. There was a big open group crit for the whole school. I brought my painting. It was quite a large, like six by eight feet, something like that. I brought it up to the crit room,... leaned it against the wall, and went across the street to have a beer. When I came back, everybody else had brought their paintings into the room and an even bigger painting was covering mine. They all overlapped, and Guston was ranting and raving and walking back and forth saying that there wasn't anything to look at, the work was all terrible, trashing everything. I thought, "Thank God, my painting is covered up!" [They laugh.] So as the crit ended, and people took their work out of the room, my painting was uncovered. Guston loved it! Went on and on about how wonderful it was. He came over to my studio to see what I was doing. Took me very seriously, very, very supportive. His enthusiasm really had a tremendous impact on me in a very negative way. It made that particular effort stand out as some kind of masterpiece or something, suggesting to me that in this particular work I had managed to keep all the balls in the air. Whereas all my other works were fatally flawed in some basic way. I realized years later—and actually I told Guston about it when later we taught together—that he had practically

137

crippled me by liking that painting so much. Certainly not his fault, but the net effect was that I spent the next four years trying to repaint that one painting.

What was the painting, by the way?

A seated nude with arms raised. It looks to me now like a pretty standard work for the time. But at any particular moment, nuance is everything....

◀ ◀ ◀

[At Yale] I probably fit in a little better than others. Serra was definitely aggressive and confrontational. It was an interesting time too, because there was the notion that the art world was basically a man's world. Nancy Graves first showed her work using the name Andrew Stevenson Graves, because she did not want to be dealt with as a woman. We used to joke that the women had more balls than the men. It was a much harder row to hoe, so they had to make bigger paintings. They had to be more aggressive and stronger. The school was about fifty-fifty women and men, and the female students were certainly a force to be dealt with. Many of them wanted to take the same route [as the men] and be professionals. It wasn't something they were doing while they were waiting to meet a man....

◀ ◀ ◀

Al Held, probably more than anybody else [teaching at Yale], was responsible for so many of us going to New York. Most of us argued violently with him all the time that we were in school. There were times when I locked him out of my studio. He was very intrusive and wanted to suggest solutions to your paintings that you didn't want to hear, and often he would try to paint on your stuff. Once he stapled some paper to one of my paintings to show me what a white area in there would look like, and I found that kind of outrageous. But Al talked about going to New York, talked about laying your neck on the line, talked about being measured by the only yardstick that mattered. You could go back to your small town, wherever it was, and be a provincial success, show in local exhibits, but if you really wanted to be an artist, you needed to go where the work would be measured by the highest standards. He talked about what New York was like and what it was like to find a loft. He talked about how to support yourself.

◀ ◀ ◀

When we [Close and his wife, Leslie Rose] arrived New York [in 1967], I used to help Richard Serra build his lead sculptures, prop them up and stuff. He used to come to my studio and look at my work, and I would go and look at his. It was—at least for me—an important time in my life as a young artist. I remember something Richard said about how to end up making work that didn't look like anybody else's, which now seems kind of curiously out of date with today's interest in appropria- tion and the ease with which one raids the cultural icebox. But at the time, I think everyone wanted to separate himself or herself from every- one else and not have the work look like art. That was the whole appeal of going to Canal Street [where buildings were being demolished] to find materials that had never been used before to make art, so that the materials came without any art-world association and no particular way to use them. Nobody wanted to work in bronze. Now everyone's making bronze sculptures. Then, anyone working in bronze was consid- ered just hopelessly lost. So you would try to find rubber, and you would see what it could do. You'd bounce it, lean it, stack it, scrunch it—what- ever you could do with it. I remember once (in terms of this notion of extremism or whatever) when Richard was talking to me about my work, he said, "You know, if you really want to separate yourself from everyone else, it's very easy. You don't even have to think. Every time you come to a fork in the road, automatically one of those two routes is going to be a harder route to take than the other. So automatically take the hardest route, because everybody else is taking the easiest route. If you take the least likely, most extreme, most bizarre, hair-shirt, rocks- in-your-shoes kind of position… you will make idiosyncratic work. You

Chuck Close

will push yourself into a particular corner that no one else occupies."
I think that was very much about what the times were like.

How did you take that when you first heard it?

I thought it was interesting advice for somebody who was now making paintings that took months and months just putting thinned-down, watery black paint on canvases and slowly building this imagery in a sort of odd, somewhat mechanical way.

[Talking about his fingerprint paintings]... I rolled a color—oil-based ink—onto the glass and picked it up with my fingers, feeling the relative surface tension of the ink, feeling how much I was picking up and then feeling how much I was putting down. Building a very complicated and randomly dispersed image either in black ink on the white canvas to make black finger paintings, or red, yellow, and blue to make color finger paintings.

It sounds very sensual.

Yes. And very physical. Physicality has had a lot more to do with the paintings than anybody thinks. Part of the problem of understanding the painting is just how physically engaged I was in making them, because they appeared to have just happened, which is what I wanted. I wanted them to look effortless. I didn't want them to look like I had labored on them for twelve or fourteen months. Because the paint was so thin, the record of my activity was so ethereal, it was impossible to tell in many cases where the artist's hand had been. I wanted to get the evidence of the artist's hand out of there. But they, were always, were very physical. I was always up to my ears in paint and very much manhandling and manipulating the surface. Now, with the finger paintings, it was possible for everyone to see just how physical an experience it was. The physicality was very important, as was the personal mark. This is my actual body. I also didn't have to feel through the tool. One of the reasons that I got brushes the hell out of the paintings in the first place was that it was like taking a shower with a raincoat on. It felt like there was something between me and the activity. You had to feel through the brush. People who feel through the brush the best have great wrists. I didn't want to make paintings that were about great wrist control. I wanted to make paintings that were about a visual experience and about the head as well as the hands. It was nice to make paintings that were unabashedly personal marks and very physical. Right now I am returning to making paintings with brushes and palettes. I just hope that I've put enough miles on me—enough years of thinking differently about the building of color—that I don't fall back into the same old color habits and the laziness. I have a new reason to look for color, and therefore I'll find it in a different place. So I'm enjoying the nostalgic smell of oil paint in my studio and holding onto the brushes. I'm even enjoying the palette… both physically and optically, I'm trying to respond to the colors on the canvas and to put down a color that isn't what I want and moving along an unlikely route to where I do want it and trying to leave that on the canvas for everybody to see.

Chuck Close

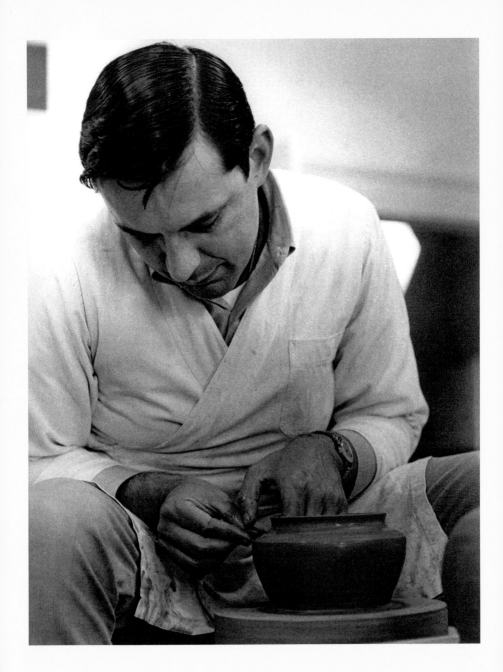

Ken Shores

Born 1928

In 2000 the Archives of American Art received a generous
grant from Nanette L. Laitman for the Nanette L. Laitman
Documentation Project for Craft and Decorative Arts in
America. The project now includes more than 150 oral history
interviews with artists working in clay, glass, fiber, metal,
and wood.

*   As part of this project, in 2007 Mija Riedel interviewed*
Ken Shores, a ceramic artist, teacher, and leader in the studio
craft movement in the Northwest. Here, Shores talks about the
"magical" properties of clay.

Ken Shores throwing a pot, ca. 1965. Photographer unknown. Courtesy of Ken Shores.

Mija Riedel: You have used clay in so many different ways, from the early functional work to very organic forms…. You've done with clay pretty much everything one can do.

Ken Shores: Yes. The various techniques require, sometimes, a different sort of clay and certainly a different approach…. And each technique has its own drawbacks and its own problems…. [That's] what makes clay interesting, because you face new challenges each time. I find clay a fascinating material. I started as a painter and then succumbed to the charisma of clay. I still do paint some and sketch, but I can't imagine replacing clay as a material for communication.

Clay I think is such a magical material, and that sounds like a cliché; but it's a material that is so responsive and has so much life to it, I don't know of any other that has that quality…. Metal is beautiful, but it's cold and unresponsive. You have to heat it, hammer it, beat it to make it bow to your wishes. Fibers are more flexible, but they tend to be lifeless until you actually get something going with them. Paint is kind of an innocuous substance; and painting is really about making two dimensions become three dimensions in the eye of the viewer. This takes a great deal of insight and talent, but the material itself is not as stunning and as human as clay, in my opinion.

Clay has that warmth of being able to say things. A mere fingerprint in clay becomes an object in itself, just touching clay. And it's so manageable, but yet, it has its restrictions. You can take it so far and torture it—when overworked, clay actually does tire out, slump, and die. It has to be dried out and rejuvenated. So clay can be a life force, but it can expire quickly if it's badly put together, eventually cracking and drying, or certainly cracking in firing. It has the last word. You think you can get by with something, but you can't, not with clay. You have to handle and treat it with respect; as a result, it will respect your wishes and come through the kiln.

I used to tell the students to treat clay… as you would an animal or person, because you almost have to talk to it and respond to it, certainly do its wishes, and yes to control it too. And clay can be controlled, especially on the wheel. Beginning students have a hard time with the wheel. They torture the clay, and they are just not able to control it, … but then they begin to work with the clay and understand how much they can move it into the center of the wheel without pushing it all the way over and throwing it off center; how they can touch it, open it up, work with the momentum of the wheel and not against it. They actually have to consider becoming acquainted with clay, and treat it like they would a friend, a human being. Now this is maybe a kind of silly analogy but it seems to work with a lot of students. At first they think, oh, that's easy to do, I'll just plunge in and do it, and then they realize that the clay deserves discipline and respect. I've encountered no other material with those attributes.

Ken Shores

Maya Lin

Born 1959

As a senior at Yale University in 1981, Maya Lin entered the national competition to design the Vietnam Veterans Memorial to be built in Washington, D.C. When she learned that her proposal—one of 1,421—had won, her initial response was, "You've got to be kidding." In the two years that it took to complete the monument, she managed to maintain the integrity of her concept in an atmosphere of intense political conflict.

The monument officially opened on November 13, 1982. Four months later, Robert Brown interviewed Lin for the Archives of American Art. In this segment, she talks about the site and the evolution of her ideas about honoring those who served and died in the Vietnam War.

Maya Lin: It was a beautiful park, wonderful. It was a sunny day, much like today. There were people playing frisbee. A memorial is supposed to respect life, basically. You're memorializing the dead, and respecting the living. You don't kill a living park to make a memorial. You don't go in there and pave it over with marble and concrete and make something so urban in a site that is so beautiful. And if, instead of fighting with the landscape, fighting and trying to overcome it, you work with it, you end up with something far stronger. So while I was at the site, I started imagining: what is a war? what is death? Death is a very painful loss, an initial violence, like a wound that heals over with time like a scar, but is never quite forgotten. You can never quite forget someone you've loved who has died. So the idea of actually making a cut into the earth, taking a knife and just opening up the earth, that's like the initial violence of war. And then you let time and the grass heal it over. And from that comes the black granite, it's like a geode, a stone that you cut and then polish its edge. You've got the rough and the sharp, knife-edge finish, and it's beautiful. The tension between that shininess and the rough, uncut outer surface is what I was looking for—literally opening the earth and polishing its edges. You know that when you polish dirt, it becomes dark black and you see on into infinity....

What about your work's neighbors? The Washington Monument, a great obelisk; and the Lincoln Memorial, a Greek temple?

It was perfect, because after you open up the earth, you have to have those legs on an angle, pointing to something: one points to the Lincoln and one to the Washington. You go down there [into the space where her memorial is situated], and it becomes a journey into your own, private world. As you walk down in there, everyone gets quieter and quieter and more removed. No matter how many people are there, you're still alone with your thoughts. That's what the area does to you. It's very somber, very sobering. And then as you turn to go out, after seeing the names and the dates, and realizing that this is a memorial to Vietnam veterans [and their dead comrades]—your present or your immediate past—you turn to walk away, and the Lincoln and Washington memorials are right there, symbols of our country. The Vietnam Memorial really ties the whole area together, architecturally and visually, which it must do, since the other monuments are such strong elements. And for me, symbolically and historically, they are our past, while the Vietnam Memorial is our present. And then you walk out, and that is your future. It's like a story being told.

You can never describe the Vietnam memorial by taking a picture of it, really. You have to walk through it. It is an experience. It's something each person has to go through. It's like a timeline. You go in, searching for an answer. You can find the answer within yourself after confronting this incredible wall of names. And then you have to walk out on your own. And that's how you accept the war and the loss. I mean, if someone who's very close to you dies, no consolation from the outside is going to make you feel better. At some point, somewhere inside of you, you have to accept that these people are *gone*, period. And then life goes on, you go on, and you're left with memories of that person....

So many people would prefer an incredibly *happy* memorial. How do you make people happy? Do you make them pretend that something that was incredibly painful for them, an incredibly powerful part of their life didn't happen? Do you just zap them with an electrode and say, "*Uh! Never Happened.* It's a beautiful day, are you happy"? Or do you say, "Look, it did happen, you suffered through a lot, you've a lot to be proud of. Remember it all. Sort it out, accept it, put it behind you, but never forget it." Because to fight, survive, or die in Vietnam was a supreme sacrifice, and the veterans who returned should be very proud of what they went through and not made to feel like, "Oh, let's put it away, it was a bad time in our history, it embarrasses everyone. Let's forget about it, let's pretend it never happened." Which is why the whole controversy really bothered me. Because I saw so many politicians trying to erase

Maya Lin

history and make the Vietnam conflict appear like *any* other war. No, it was a *different* war. It caused a lot more pain and a lot more trouble for the veterans. The soldiers who came back were not forgiven for their country's war. *They* became the victims, *they* became the people who did the killing, *they* had to take it in and absorb it personally.

Did you arrive at your design fairly early in the process?
Yes. Basically I was playing around with greens, and I just made a slash in the earth. And that's the memorial. And then all kinks were worked out, literally—the names, and how they were to be listed—alphabetically? chronologically? I hated the alphabetical listing. It's so bureaucratic, it's so cold. You have a million Smiths in one place. It's not how they died. It shouldn't be how they are remembered. At Yale [University], my freshman year, a little old man was still carving names onto Woolsey Hall—a huge marble rotunda where all of the Yale men who were killed in wars are listed. They're carved in one by one, chiseled in, in chronological order. And the date's listed. When you can touch those names on the wall in the order in which they died, it is so much more significant. And that's how I knew that, in my work, the list of the dead had to be chronological. If I'd had my way, and if enough money and time had been allotted, I would have had those walls erected and then had each name carved, one by one, in the order in which people died. That would take a long time to do. But those men gave their lives; they gave up everything for that war. [The names were not carved by hand, but by a computerized typesetting process called photo stencil grit blasting.]

You had that idea, yourself, by winter of '81 or so?
The assignment was made in late November [1981]. On December 20, I think, I took my proposal before . . . a panel of about five professors. For the preliminary review, I carried in these two walls, one pointing to the Lincoln, one pointing to the Washington. I assumed that the names would be put down chronologically, beginning at one end, ending at another. Our professor looked at me and said, "That won't go, because

you come to the end, the strongest part is the middle, and what have you got? An arbitrary middle point where the names are. You have to make that the strongest point." The professor, Andy Burr, was totally right. I presented first at the reviews. By end of the class, I said, "Andy, I've got it. It's got to be beginning and end, a circle coming to a close, being broken by the earth." And he looked at me and said, "You're right."

… So you've got beginning and end coming together and meeting. [The names are in chronological order: for the dead, according to the date of casualty; for the missing, the date when they were reported missing. The list starts and ends at the middle of the monument.] The war ends. Reconciliation can only take place after there is an end. Beginning and end meet. The war is complete.

Guerrilla Girls

Est. 1985

In 2007 the Archives of American Art began a series of
interviews with sixteen members of the Guerrilla Girls, a
group of radical feminists established in New York City in
1985 primarily to promote women artists through posters,
performances, and other forms of political activism. They
are anonymous rebels. Each member assumes the name of
a deceased woman artist and in public performances wears
a gorilla mask to hide her true identity.

As feminism has evolved, so has the group. There are
now three main factions: Guerrilla Girls, Inc.; Guerrilla Girls
On Tour, Inc.; and Guerrilla Girls Broad Band, Inc. These
interviews present multiple and occasionally conflicting
recollections of their collective struggle for social change, as well
as their individual points of view. To protect their anonymity,
interviewer Judith Richards signed a non-disclosure agreement
before she conducted the face-to-face interviews.

Guerrilla Girl "Aphra Behn" encounters a police officer while protesting the Tony Awards,
New York City, 1999. On her cape is written, "There's a tragedy on Broadway and it's not Electra."
Courtesy of the Guerrilla Girls.

Guerrilla Girl 1: You know, let me tell you something. We started in 1985, after… the Museum of Modern Art opened with a sculpture and painting show ["An International Survey of Recent Painting and Sculpture," May 17–August 19, 1984]. Kynaston McShine… organized that. There were 166 people in the show, or 169, because there were some groups, and thirteen were women. Hell, this is— and no women of color.

Rosalba Carriera: Well, that's what started it.

GG 1: We said, you know, "This is completely out of line." And there were protests; women were protesting outside the museum, to say, you know, this is not the way it should be. And, of course, they always use the line "Well, you know, we really have standards"; that's why women are not in it. You know, that old adage that is just bullshit. And, frankly, the show was not that impressive, anyway, which I hate to say, but, nevertheless, it wasn't. But the fact that so many people were left out at that time, when the Modern reopened in '84, made a lot of women angry.

RC: … But what we did, in reaction to that, we had our own show at the Palladium ["The Night the Palladium Apologized," at the Palladium nightclub, New York, 1985].

GG 1: That's correct, yes.

RC: Because, at that time, the clubs downtown were showcases for what was going on in art. You know, Keith Haring was doing things there, and Jean-Michel Basquiat was doing things there. It was basically the young, rebellious guys. So, the Guerrilla Girls put on a show at the Palladium, and that was my first entry into the Guerrilla Girls, that night, because a big painting of mine was in it, I joined the Guerrilla Girls. I thought, "Wow, this is great" [laughs].

GG 1: This *is* great [laughs].

RC: …And it was a great night, because instead of seeing all this young male energy, there were all these great paintings by women, and everybody was dancing, and it was that heaviness of the club scene and it was like women's art, instead of art by the bad boys…. It was a thrill. … And, you know, that was all part of the '80s, the decadence and the excesses of the '80s, the clubs, and you know how the male artists were, like, smoking cigars and wearing Italian suits and hanging out at Mr. Chow's and, going to the big, fancy dinners, and all that stuff.

And so we didn't want to come across like Birkenstock feminists and like, "Well, we're holding our babies in one hand, but we really want our due." [Guerrilla Girl 1 laughs.] That's why we tried to look—you know, we wore black—kind of sexy and more hard-edged, to get people's attention.
GG 1: Yes.
RC: … Not to say that we didn't have babies at home, or any of that, but this wasn't the face we wanted to present. We wanted to show that we're out in this world, we're hip, we're cool, we're funny, and we are doing it.

◁ ◁ ◁

RC: I am active in lots of things that are not the Guerrilla Girls at this point. The Guerrilla Girls has given me the power within myself to speak my beliefs. I think that is, like, an amazing thing.
GG 1: You know something? It really *is* amazing, the fact that—just to be able to say— to be empowered to say something direct, not always with anger, but just basically, "This is the situation, and it has to change."
RC: And not only in groups. I mean, I find in my everyday dealings, because they far outstretch the bounds of the art world right now—that I am—I mean, I have heard people say that I am a force to be reckoned with. I know that happened by being a Guerrilla Girl. It really, really empowered me.

◁ ◁ ◁

Gertrude Stein: Another story that I don't think anybody knows is where the gorilla mask came from. "Rosalba Carriera" came up with the idea of honoring dead women artists by using their names. But an early, early member—it was before we were taking the names of dead women artists, anyway—she was taking notes at the first or second meeting, or something.... Anyway, she wrote "Gorilla Girls," G-O-R-I-L-L-A G-I-R-L-S. And then somebody thought, "Oh, gorilla girls," and the mask came right out of this misspelling.

Alice Neel: ... I remember that, because there was a lot of turmoil about whether we should align ourselves with the guerrillas, the real guerrillas who are fighting, you know, what is that saying about—

> **Judith Richards:** Do you mean [that the group's name was supposed to] be spelled "Gorilla Girls?"

AN: Yes.

GS: Right, right.

AN: How do we spell it? . . .

◀ ◀ ◀

For the opening of the downtown Guggenheim at 575 Broadway at Prince Street in 1992, the museum staff was planning an exhibition including works by Constantin Brancusi, Wassily Kandinsky, Joseph Beuys, Carl Andre, and Robert Ryman.

In this segment, "Gertrude Stein" and "Alice Neel" recall the Guerrilla Girls' successful campaign to broaden the exhibition. As a result of their actions, Louise Bourgeois was added to the show.

GS: Okay. The downtown Guggenheim was cranking up. Their first show was Carl Andre, Brancusi, somebody . . . Four white guys.

AN: Yes.

GS: So "Eva Hesse" wrote a pink postcard that said, "Dear Mr. Krens, [Thomas Krens, then the director of the Solomon R. Guggenheim Museum, New York] welcome to downtown. We have heard about your first show, 'Four White Boys of the White Boys Museum.' Lotsa luck, Guerrilla Girls," and then we printed up thousands of these cards.

AN: Yes. Oh, that's right, yes [laughs].

GS: And then we handed them out to galleries and members and people.... And then they mailed the cards to Tom Krens. And then the Guggenheim put Louise Bourgeois in that show [and changed the title to: "From Brancusi to Bourgeois: Aspects of the Guggenheim Collection," held June 28–September 6, 1992].

AN: And that was credit to the Guerrilla Girls....

GS: ...And then, the night of the opening—

AN: Bourgeois was the token woman.... The best artist, too, in the group.

GS: The WAC [Women's Action Coalition] drum corps came around...and we gave out...paper bags, so everybody could be a Guerrilla Girl.

AN: Right.

GS: And then there was a protest about Ana Mendieta, wasn't there?

AN: Yes,...at the same time.... Because she wasn't represented in the show, and the whole thing about her—

GS: —Well, because Carl Andre [the late Mendieta's husband] was in the show.

AN: There was the murder thing. [Mendieta fell to her death from a 34th-floor apartment on September 8, 1985. Andre was subsequently tried for her murder and acquitted.]

GS: Right, right.

AN: —and the whole, you know, suspicion and all.

GS: So—

AN: So that night we merged with WAC.... It was like this big group.

GS: It was a huge collaboration. It was probably the first and last time we ever did anything with WAC.

AN: That we worked together with another group.

GS: But, because there were some members going back and forth.... There was communication between the groups, and we planned this thing. And it was just a huge success.

AN: Yes.

GS: We stopped traffic on Broadway.

AN: Right

GS: The place was completely filled with bodies.

AN: The paper-bag masks were great.... The card was terrific—

GS: —People couldn't get in. It was so—

AN: Yes.

GS: You know, people were jamming themselves into this space.

AN: Yes. It was very good. Yes, it was exciting.

GS: And so we changed art history. That would be—

AN: We did.

GS: —my proudest memory.

◀ ◀ ◀

[Referring to the group in the mid-1990s] You're implying that, possibly, new members weren't involved as visual artists, and therefore there wasn't the skill, talent, and passion about a visual solution—

AN: I don't know if it was because it [the collective energy to focus on specific issues] was visual. It might have been.... I think—I thought, too, that maybe this was the time for the Guerrilla Girls to—I always had a fantasy of a sort of going back to the jungle, or whatever you want to say, and reemerging as this sort of a union for artists.

At this point, I still grapple with it, except that I do see that—especially recently, from the work of "Gertrude [Stein]" and "Frida [Kahlo]" and the [various Guerrilla Girl] groups, that there is still a life for the group, and a really important place for it, you know. I'm sort of switching my idea about the value of it, as a result of our having received an award at the Brooklyn Museum, which was very interesting. [The Guerrilla Girls received the Brooklyn Museum Women in the Arts Award in 2007]

But I do feel that maybe this is the time…to sort of let it kind of rest and reemerge in some other form, or another way. I think the group has had an incredible impact, and I think its life has maybe now shifted, or is in transition in some way. I don't know what that is, you know. I am so interested in hearing the voice of younger women. I want to hear their voice, you know, what they have to say about it, because they're in a whole different generation—

GS: —And their views about feminism are completely different.

AN: Very different.

GS: Yes.

AN: And I think it has to reemerge as theirs—they have to do it.

GS: Yes.

AN: They have to take over.

GS: Yes.

Published by

 Smithsonian
Archives of American Art

aaa.si.edu

 **WINTERHOUSE
EDITIONS**

winterhouse.com

ISBN 10: 1-884381-24-3
ISBN 13: 978-1-884381-24-9

Design: Winterhouse
Editor: Susan F. Rossen
Printing: Finlay Printing

Published with the support of the Dedalus Foundation, Inc.